$\mathscr{E}$ASY

$\mathscr{W}$EDDING $\mathscr{P}$LANNING

The Most Comprehensive and
Informative Wedding
Planner Available
Today!

Concise and Easy to Read

By
Elizabeth & Alex Lluch
Professional Wedding Consultants

Written by Elizabeth & Alex Lluch
Professional Wedding Consultants

Published by Wedding Solutions Publishing, Inc.
© Copyright 2000

Reviewed and Approved by:
Wilda Hyer,
California State Coordinator for the Association of Bridal Consultants; Owner of *Events Plus,* Ceres, California;
and
Gayle Labenow,
New York Metro Coordinator for the Association of Bridal Consultants; Owner of *You Are Cordially Invited,* Babylon, New York.

Front Cover Photos provided by:

top left:	top mid, right, bottom:
Jon Barber	Karen French
Barber Photography	*Karen French Photography*
34085 Pacific Coast Hwy #117	8351 Elmcrest
Dana Point, CA 92629	Huntington Beach, CA 92646
(949) 493-5840	(800) 734-6219

Back Cover Photos provided by:
Jon Barber (top) & Karen French (middle & bottom)

Cover Design by: Amy Allen Graphics, San Diego, CA

Printed in USA

ISBN #1-887169-12-1
3rd Edition

*T*HE WEDDING OF

_____

&

_____

*W*HO WILL BE MARRIED ON

_____

*A*T

_____

DEDICATED TO:

All brides and grooms.
May their wedding day be the
happiest day of their life!

$\mathscr{C}$ONTENTS

*I*NTRODUCTION

*D*ear Bride and Groom:

Congratulations on your engagement! You must be very excited for having found that special person to share the rest of your life with. And you must be looking forward to what will be the happiest day of your life -- your wedding! Planning your wedding can be fun and exciting. But it can also be very stressful. That is why Wedding Solutions Publishing, Inc., a professional wedding planning company, created *Easy Wedding Planning*.

Easy Wedding Planning has helped many couples plan the wedding of their dreams. This book has enabled them to attend their wedding feeling relaxed, knowing that all the plans and details of their wedding have been taken care of.

Easy Wedding Planning begins with a very detailed wedding planning checklist containing everything you need to do or consider when planning your wedding and the best time frame in which to accomplish each activity. Each item in the checklist is followed by the page number(s) where that item is explained within the book.

The checklist is followed by a comprehensive and detailed budget analysis, listing all the expenses that are typically incurred in a wedding as well as the percentage of the total budget that is typically spent in each category. Each expense item in the budget is followed by the page number(s) where that item is explained within the book. This makes it very easy to find detailed information on each item.

The budget analysis is followed by a detailed description of each item in the budget including: Options, Things To Consider, Questions To Ask, Things To Beware Of, Tips To Save Money, and Price Ranges. Our clients find this format to be both informative and easy to use, and we know you will too!

Next is a short chapter on Wedding Traditions, explaining the symbolic meaning and historical purpose of some of the more common wedding traditions, and a list of "Do's" and "Don'ts" when planning your wedding.

We have included a list of responsibilities for each member of your wedding party as well as the traditional formations for the ceremony, processional, recessional and receiving line for both Jewish and Christian weddings. We have also included traditional seating arrangements at the reception.

Lastly, new to this edition is a complete Honeymoon Planner to help you plan and budget for the honeymoon of your dreams. You will find everything, from destination ideas and telephone contacts, to packing checklists and budgeting tips.

We are confident that you will enjoy planning your wedding with the help of *Easy Wedding Planning*. So come join the many couples who have used this book to plan a stress-free wedding. Also, if you know other options, things to consider, tips to save money, or anything else that you would like to see included in this book, please write to us at: Wedding Solutions Publishing, Inc.; 6347 Caminito Tenedor; San Diego, CA 92120. We will include your ideas or suggestions in our next printing. We listen to brides and grooms like you -- that is why *Easy Wedding Planning* has become the best wedding planning book available!

Sincerely,

Elizabeth H. Lluch

𝒲EDDING 𝒫LANNING 𝒞HECKLIST

This Wedding Planning Checklist itemizes everything you need to do or consider when planning your wedding, and the best time frame in which to accomplish each activity.

As you can see, many of the items are followed by the page number(s) where those items are explained in more detail within the book. This will help you find the information you need, when you need it.

This checklist assumes that you have nine months or more to plan your wedding. If your wedding is in less than nine months, just start at the beginning of the list and try to catch up as quickly as you can!

Use the boxes to the left of the items to check-off the activities as you accomplish them. This will enable you to see your progress and help you determine what has been done and what still needs to be done.

This comprehensive Wedding Planning Checklist is also available as a large poster (9.5" x 23") which can be mounted on any surface such as a wall, refrigerator, door or mirror. This attractive and convenient poster allows you to see, at a glance, your wedding planning progress.

This checklist is available through Wedding Solutions Publishing, Inc. for $5.95. As a special offer to our readers, you may order it free of charge. Simply send $2.95 for shipping and handling to Wedding Solutions Publishing, Inc.; 6347 Caminito Tenedor, San Diego, CA 92120.

Nine Months and Earlier	*Page*
❑ Announce your engagement.	
❑ Select a date for your wedding.	
❑ Hire a professional wedding consultant.	178
❑ Determine the type of wedding you want: location, formality, time of day, number of guests, etc.	37
❑ Determine budget and how expenses will be shared.	25, 27
❑ Develop a record-keeping system for payments made.	219
❑ Consolidate all guest lists: bride's, groom's, bride's family, groom's family, and organize as follows: 1) those who must be invited 2) those who should be invited 3) those who would be nice to invite	
❑ Decide if you want to include children among guests.	
❑ Select and reserve ceremony site.	37, 38
❑ Select and reserve your officiant.	39
❑ Select and reserve reception site.	103

Nine **Months and Earlier (Cont.)**	*Page*
❑ Select and order your bridal gown and headpiece.	45
❑ Determine your color scheme.	
❑ Send engagement notice with a photograph to your local newspaper.	68
❑ Buy a calendar and note all important activities: showers, luncheons, parties, get-togethers, etc.	171
❑ If ceremony or reception is at home, arrange for home or garden improvements as needed.	
❑ Order passport, visa or birth certificate, if needed for your honeymoon or marriage license.	299
❑ Select and book photographer.	59
❑ Select maid of honor, best man, bridesmaids and ushers (approx. one usher per 50 guests).	195

Six to Nine Months Before Wedding	Page
❏ Select flower girl and ring bearer.	204, 205
❏ Give the *Wedding Party Responsibility Cards* to your wedding party.	195
❏ Reserve wedding night bridal suite.	
❏ Select attendants' dresses, shoes and accessories.	
❏ Select flower girl's dress, shoes and accessories.	
❏ Select and book caterer, if needed.	107
❏ Select and book ceremony musicians.	121
❏ Select and book reception musicians or DJ.	123
❏ Schedule fittings and delivery dates for yourself, attendants, flower girl and ring bearer.	
❏ Select and book videographer.	71
❏ Select and book florist.	133

Four to Six Months Before Wedding	*Page*
❏ Start shopping for each other's wedding gifts.	167
❏ Reserve rental items needed for ceremony & reception.	159
❏ Finalize guest list.	
❏ Select and order wedding invitations, announcements and other stationery such as thank-you notes, wedding programs, and seating cards.	77
❏ Address invitations or hire a calligrapher.	94
❏ Set date, time and location for your rehearsal dinner.	171
❏ Arrange accommodations for out-of-town guests.	
❏ Start planning your honeymoon.	
❏ Select and book all miscellaneous services, i.e. gift attendant, valet parking, etc.	119
❏ Register for gifts.	
❏ Purchase shoes & accessories.	50
❏ Begin to break-in your shoes.	52

$\mathcal{T}$wo to Four Months Before Wedding	$\mathcal{P}$age
❑ Select bakery and order wedding cake.	127
❑ Order party favors.	116
❑ Select and order room decorations.	153
❑ Purchase honeymoon attire & luggage.	
❑ Select and book transportation for wedding day.	155
❑ Check blood test and marriage license requirements.	174
❑ Shop for wedding rings and engrave them.	
❑ Consider having your teeth cleaned or bleached.	
❑ Consider writing a will and/or pre-nuptial agreement.	175
❑ Plan activities for your out-of-town guests both before and after the wedding.	
❑ Purchase gifts for wedding attendants.	168, 169

Six to Eight Weeks Before Wedding	*Page*
❑ Mail invitations. Include accommodation choices and a map to assist guests in finding the ceremony and reception sites.	77, 89
❑ Maintain a record of RSVPs and all gifts received. Send thank-you notes upon receipt of gifts.	93
❑ Determine hair style and makeup. Have hairdresser work with your headpiece.	53
❑ Schedule to have your hair, makeup and nails done the day of the wedding.	53, 54
❑ Finalize shopping for wedding day accessories such as toasting glasses, ring pillow, guest book, etc.	41, 42, 131
❑ Set up an area or a table in your home to display gifts as you receive them.	
❑ Check with your local newspapers for wedding announcement requirements.	173
❑ Have your formal wedding portrait taken.	69

Six to Eight Weeks Before Wedding (Cont.)	*Page*
❑ Send wedding announcement & photograph to your local newspapers.	173
❑ Change name & address on drivers license, social security card, insurance policies, subscriptions, bank accounts, memberships, etc.	
❑ Select and reserve wedding attire for groom, ushers, father of the bride and ring bearer.	55
❑ Select a guest book attendant. Decide where and when to have guests sign in.	41
❑ Mail invitations to rehearsal dinner.	171
❑ Get blood test and health certificate.	174
❑ Obtain marriage license.	174
❑ Plan a luncheon or dinner with your bridesmaids. Give them their gifts at that time or at the rehearsal dinner.	171
❑ Find "something old, something new, something borrowed, something blue, and a six pence (or shiny penny) for your shoe."	184
❑ Finalize your menu, beverage and alcohol order with your caterer.	107, 110, 113

$\mathcal{T}$wo to Six Weeks Before Wedding	$\mathcal{P}$age
☐ Confirm ceremony details with your officiant.	38
☐ Arrange final fitting of bridesmaids' dresses.	
☐ Have final fitting of your gown and headpiece.	49
☐ Finalize rehearsal dinner plans; arrange seating and write names on place cards, if desired.	88
☐ Make final floral selections.	133
☐ Make a detailed schedule for your wedding party.	
☐ Make a detailed schedule for your service providers.	
☐ Confirm details with all service providers, including attire. Give them a copy of your wedding schedule.	
☐ Start packing for your honeymoon.	
☐ Finalize addressing and stamping announcements.	93
☐ Decide if you want to form a receiving line. If so, determine when and where to form the line.	188

*T*wo to Six Weeks Before Wedding (Cont.)	*P*age
❏ Contact guests who haven't responded.	
❏ Pick up rings and check for fit.	
❏ Meet with photographer and confirm special photos you want taken.	61
❏ Meet with videographer and confirm special events or people you want videotaped.	71
❏ Meet with musicians and confirm music to be played during special events such as first dance.	121
❏ Continue writing thank-you notes as gifts arrive.	93
❏ Remind bridesmaids and ushers of when and where to pick up their wedding attire.	
❏ Purchase the lipstick, nail polish and any other accessories you want your bridesmaids to wear.	168
❏ Determine ceremony seating for special guests. Give a list to the ushers.	
❏ Plan reception room layout and seating with your reception site manager or caterer. Write names on place cards for arranged seating.	88

The Last Week	Page
❏ Pick up wedding attire and make sure everything fits.	
❏ Do final guest count and notify your caterer or reception site manager.	107
❏ Gather everything you will need for the rehearsal and wedding day as listed in the *Wedding Party Responsibility Cards*.	215
❏ Arrange for someone to drive the getaway car.	197
❏ Review the schedule of events and last minute arrangements with your service providers.	
❏ Confirm all honeymoon reservations and accommodations. Pick up tickets and travelers checks.	227
❏ Finish packing your suitcases for the honeymoon.	289
❏ Familiarize yourself with guests' names. It will help during the receiving line and reception.	
❏ Have the Post Office hold your mail while you are away on your honeymoon.	

The Rehearsal Day	*Page*
❑ Review list of things to bring to the rehearsal as listed in the *Wedding Party Responsibility Cards*.	215
❑ Put suitcases in getaway car.	
❑ Give your bridesmaids the lipstick, nail polish and accessories you want them to wear for the wedding.	168
❑ Give best man the officiant's fee and any other checks for service providers. Instruct him to deliver these checks the day of the wedding.	
❑ Arrange for someone to bring accessories such as flower basket, ring pillow, guest book & pen, toasting glasses, cake cutting knife and napkins to the ceremony and reception.	
❑ Arrange for someone to mail announcements the day after the wedding.	93
❑ Arrange for someone to return rental items such as tuxedos, slip and cake pillars after the wedding.	159
❑ Provide each member of your wedding party with a detailed schedule of events for the wedding day.	
❑ Review ceremony seating with ushers.	

The Wedding Day	*Page*
❑ Review list of things to bring to the ceremony as listed in the *Wedding Party Responsibility Cards*.	216
❑ Give the groom's ring to the maid of honor. Give the bride's ring to the best man.	196, 197
❑ Simply follow your detailed schedule of events.	
❑ Relax and enjoy your wedding!	

$\mathscr{B}$UDGET $\mathscr{A}$NALYSIS

This comprehensive Budget Analysis has been designed to provide you with all the expenses that can be incurred in any size wedding, including such hidden costs as taxes, gratuities and other "items" that can easily add up to thousands of dollars in a wedding. After you have completed this budget, you will have a much better idea of what your wedding will cost. You can then prioritize and allocate your expenses accordingly.

This budget is divided into fifteen categories: Ceremony, Wedding Attire, Photography, Videography, Stationery, Reception, Music, Bakery, Flowers, Decorations, Transportation, Rental Items, Gifts, Parties, and Miscellaneous. Categories or items written in italics are typically paid for by the groom or his family.

At the beginning of each category is the percentage of your wedding budget that is typically spent in that category, based on national averages. Multiply your intended wedding budget by this percentage and write that amount in the "typical" space provided.

To determine the total cost of your wedding, estimate the amount of money you will spend on each item in the budget analysis and write that amount in the "Budget" column after each item. Next to each expense item is the page number where you can find detailed information about that item. Items printed in italics are traditionally paid for by the groom or his family.

Add all the "Budget" amounts within each category and write the total amount in the "Budget Subtotal" space at the end of each category. Then add all the "Subtotal" figures to come up with your final wedding budget. The "Actual" column is for you to input your actual expenses as you purchase items or hire your service providers. Writing down the actual expenses will help you stay within your budget.

For example, if your total wedding budget is $10,000, then write this amount at the top of page 27. To figure your typical ceremony expenses, multiply $10,000 x .05 (5%) = $500.00. Write this amount on the "Typical" line under the "Ceremony" category to serve as a guide for all your ceremony expenses.

If you find, after adding up all your "Budget Subtotals," that the total amount is more than what you had in mind to spend, simply decide which items are more important to you and adjust your expenses accordingly.

The section immediately following the Budget Analysis provides a full explanation of each item in the budget, including a full description of the item or service, options available for that item or service, things to consider when purchasing or hiring that item or service, questions to ask in order to make the best buying decision, things to beware of, tips to save money, and a price range for each item or service, based on national averages.

Budget Analysis

Your Wedding Budget $_____

CEREMONY

(Typical = 5% of Budget) $_____

	BUDGET	ACTUAL	PAGE
Ceremony Site Fee	$_____	$_____	37
Officiant's Fee	$_____	$_____	39
Officiant's Gratuity	$_____	$_____	40
Guest Book, Pen, Penholder	$_____	$_____	41
Ring Bearer Pillow	$_____	$_____	42
Flower Girl Basket	$_____	$_____	42
Subtotal 1	$_____	$_____	

WEDDING ATTIRE

(Typical = 10% of Budget) $_____

	BUDGET	ACTUAL	PAGE
Bridal Gown	$_____	$_____	45
Alterations	$_____	$_____	49
Headpiece & Veil	$_____	$_____	49

WEDDING ATTIRE (CONT.)	BUDGET	ACTUAL	PAGE
Gloves	$_____	$_____	50
Jewelry	$_____	$_____	51
Stockings	$_____	$_____	51
Garter	$_____	$_____	52
Shoes	$_____	$_____	52
Hairdresser	$_____	$_____	53
Makeup Artist	$_____	$_____	53
Manicure/Pedicure	$_____	$_____	54
Groom's Formal Wear	$_____	$_____	55
Subtotal 2	$_____	$_____	

PHOTOGRAPHY

(Typical = 9% of Budget)	$_____		
	BUDGET	ACTUAL	PAGE
Bride & Groom's Album	$_____	$_____	59
Parents' Album	$_____	$_____	65
Extra Prints	$_____	$_____	65
Proofs/Previews	$_____	$_____	66
Negatives	$_____	$_____	67
Engagement Photograph	$_____	$_____	68
Formal Bridal Portrait	$_____	$_____	69
Subtotal 3	$_____	$_____	

VIDEOGRAPHY

(Typical = 5% of Budget) $_____

	BUDGET	ACTUAL	PAGE
Main Video	$____	$____	71
Titles	$____	$____	74
Extra Hours	$____	$____	75
Photo Montage	$____	$____	75
Extra Copies	$____	$____	76
Subtotal 4	$____	$____	

STATIONERY

(Typical = 4% of Budget) $_____

	BUDGET	ACTUAL	PAGE
Invitations	$____	$____	77
Response Cards	$____	$____	84
Reception Cards	$____	$____	86
Ceremony Cards	$____	$____	87
Pew Cards	$____	$____	87
Seating/Place Cards	$____	$____	88
Rain Cards	$____	$____	89
Maps	$____	$____	89
Ceremony Programs	$____	$____	90
Announcements	$____	$____	93

STATIONERY (CONT.)	BUDGET	ACTUAL	PAGE
Thank-You Notes	$____	$____	93
Stamps	$____	$____	94
Calligraphy	$____	$____	94
Napkins and Matchbooks	$____	$____	95
Subtotal 5	$____	$____	

RECEPTION

(Typical = 35% of Budget) $_____

	BUDGET	ACTUAL	PAGE
Reception Site Fee	$____	$____	103
Hors D'oeuvres	$____	$____	106
Main Meal/Caterer	$____	$____	107
Liquor/ Beverages	$____	$____	110
Bartending/Bar Set-up Fee	$____	$____	113
Corkage Fee	$____	$____	113
Fee to Pour Coffee	$____	$____	114
Service Providers' Meals	$____	$____	114
Gratuity	$____	$____	115
Party Favors	$____	$____	116
Disposable Cameras	$____	$____	117
Rose Petals/Rice	$____	$____	118
Gift Attendant	$____	$____	119

RECEPTION (CONT.)	BUDGET	ACTUAL	PAGE
Parking Fee/Valet Services	$_____	$_____	119
Subtotal 6	$_____	$_____	

MUSIC

(Typical = 5% of Budget)	$_____		
	BUDGET	ACTUAL	PAGE
Ceremony Music	$_____	$_____	121
Reception Music	$_____	$_____	123
Subtotal 7	$_____	$_____	

BAKERY

(Typical = 2% of Budget)	$_____		
	BUDGET	ACTUAL	PAGE
Wedding Cake	$_____	$_____	127
Groom's Cake	$_____	$_____	129
Cake Delivery & Set-up Fee	$_____	$_____	130
Cake-Cutting Fee	$_____	$_____	130
Cake Top	$_____	$_____	131
Cake Knife/Toast Glasses	$_____	$_____	131
Subtotal 8	$_____	$_____	

FLOWERS

(Typical = 6% of Budget)	$_____		
	BUDGET	**ACTUAL**	**PAGE**
BOUQUETS			
Bride's	$_____	$_____	133
Tossing	$_____	$_____	138
Maid of Honor's	$_____	$_____	139
Bridesmaids'	$_____	$_____	139
FLORAL HAIRPIECE			
Maid of Honor/ Bridesmaids'	$_____	$_____	140
Flower Girl's	$_____	$_____	140
CORSAGES			
Bride's Going Away	$_____	$_____	141
Other Family Members'	$_____	$_____	142
BOUTONNIERES			
Groom's	$_____	$_____	143
Ushers and Other Family's	$_____	$_____	143
CEREMONY SITE FLOWERS			
Main Altar	$_____	$_____	144

FLOWERS (CONT.)	BUDGET	ACTUAL	PAGE
Alter Candelabra	$_____	$_____	146
Aisle Pews	$_____	$_____	146

RECEPTION SITE FLOWERS

	BUDGET	ACTUAL	PAGE
Reception Site	$_____	$_____	147
Head Table	$_____	$_____	148
Guest Tables	$_____	$_____	148
Buffet Table	$_____	$_____	149
Punch Table	$_____	$_____	150
Cake Table	$_____	$_____	150
Cake	$_____	$_____	150
Cake Knife	$_____	$_____	151
Toasting Glasses	$_____	$_____	151
Floral Delivery & Setup	$_____	$_____	151
Subtotal 9	$_____	$_____	

DECORATIONS

(Typical = 3% of Budget) $_____

	BUDGET	ACTUAL	PAGE
Table Centerpieces	$_____	$_____	153
Balloons	$_____	$_____	154
Subtotal 10	$_____	$_____	

TRANSPORTATION

(Typical = 2% of Budget)	$_____		
	BUDGET	**ACTUAL**	**PAGE**
Transportation	$_____	$_____	155
Subtotal 11	$_____	$_____	

RENTAL ITEMS

(Typical = 3% of Budget)	$_____		
	BUDGET	**ACTUAL**	**PAGE**
Bridal Slip	$_____	$_____	159
Ceremony Accessories	$_____	$_____	159
Tent/Canopy	$_____	$_____	162
Dance Floor	$_____	$_____	163
Tables/Chairs	$_____	$_____	163
Linen/Tableware	$_____	$_____	164
Heaters	$_____	$_____	165
Lanterns	$_____	$_____	165
Other	$_____	$_____	165
Subtotal 12	$_____	$_____	

GIFTS

(Typical = 3% of Budget)	$_____		
	BUDGET	**ACTUAL**	**PAGE**
Bride's Gift	$_____	$_____	167
Groom's Gift	$_____	$_____	167
Bridesmaids' Gifts	$_____	$_____	168
Ushers' Gifts	$_____	$_____	169
Subtotal 13	$_____	$_____	

PARTIES

(Typical = 4% of Budget)	$_____		
	BUDGET	**ACTUAL**	**PAGE**
Bridesmaids' Luncheon	$_____	$_____	171
Rehearsal Dinner	$_____	$_____	171
Subtotal 14	$_____	$_____	

MISCELLANEOUS

(Typical = 4% of Budget)	$_____		
	BUDGET	**ACTUAL**	**PAGE**
Newspaper Announcements	$_____	$_____	173
Marriage License	$_____	$_____	174
Prenuptial Agreement	$_____	$_____	175

MISCELLANEOUS (CONT.)	BUDGET	ACTUAL	PAGE
Bridal Gown Preservation	$_____	$_____	176
Bouquet Preservation	$_____	$_____	177
Wedding Consultant	$_____	$_____	178
Wedding Planning Software	$_____	$_____	180
Taxes	$_____	$_____	181
Subtotal 15	$_____	$_____	
TOTAL (Add "Budget" & "Actual" Subtotals 1-15")	$_____	$_____	

*C*EREMONY

CEREMONY SITE FEE

The ceremony site fee is the fee to rent a facility for your wedding. In churches, cathedrals, chapels, temples, or synagogues, this fee may include the organist, wedding coordinator, custodian, changing rooms for the bridal party, and miscellaneous items such as kneeling cushions, aisle runner, and candelabra. Be sure to ask what the site fee includes prior to booking a facility. Throughout this book, the word church will be used to refer to the site where the ceremony will take place.

Options: Churches, cathedrals, chapels, temples, synagogues, private homes, gardens, hotels, clubs, halls, parks, museums, yachts, wineries, beaches, and hot air balloons.

Things To Consider: Your selection of a ceremony site will be influenced by the formality of your wedding, the season of the year, the number of guests expected and your religious affiliation. Make sure you ask about restrictions or guidelines regarding photography, videography, music, decorations, candles, and rice or rose petal-tossing. Consider issues such as proximity of the ceremony site to the reception site, parking availability, handicapped accessibility, and time constraints.

Questions To Ask: Make sure you ask all the following questions before selecting a ceremony site:

- What is the name & phone number of my contact person?
- What dates & times are available?
- How much time will be allotted for my ceremony?
- Do vows need to be approved?
- What is the ceremony site fee?
- What is the payment policy?
- What is the cancellation policy?
- Does the facility have liability insurance?
- What are the minimum & maximum number of guests allowed?
- What is the denomination, if any, of the facility?
- What restrictions are there with regards to denomination?
- Is an officiant available? At what cost?
- Are outside officiants allowed?
- Are any musical instruments available for our use?
- If so, what is the fee?
- Are there are any music restrictions?
- Are there are any photography restrictions?
- Are there are any videography restrictions?
- Are there are any restrictions for rice or rose petal-tossing?
- Are candlelight ceremonies allowed?
- What floral decorations are available/allowed?
- When is my rehearsal to be scheduled?

- Is a dressing room available?
- Is there handicap accessibility and parking?
- How many parking spaces are available for my family & wedding party? Where are they located?
- How many parking spaces are available for my guests?
- What rental items are necessary?

Tips To Save Money: Have your ceremony at the same facility as your reception to save a second rental fee. Set a realistic guest list and stick to it. Hire an experienced wedding consultant. At a church or temple, ask if there is another wedding that day and share the cost of floral decorations with that bride. Membership in a church, temple or club can reduce rental fees. At a garden wedding, have guests stand and omit the cost of renting chairs.

Price Range: $100 - $800

OFFICIANT'S FEE

The officiant's fee is the fee paid to whomever performs your wedding ceremony.

Options: Priest, Clergyman, Minister, Pastor, Chaplain, Rabbi, Judge, or Justice of the Peace.

Discuss with your officiant the readings you would like incorporated into your ceremony. Some popular readings are:

Beatitudes	Corinthians 13:1-13
Ecclesiastes 3:1-9	Ephesians 3:14-19; 5:1-2
Genesis 1:26-28	Genesis 2:4-9, 15-24
Hosea 2:19-21	Isaiah 61:10I
John 4:7-16	John 15:9-12, 17:22-24
Mark 10:6-9	Proverbs 31:10-31
Romans 12:1-2, 9-18	Ruth 1:16-17
Song of Solomon	Tobit 8:56-58

Things To Consider: Some officiants may not accept a fee, depending on your relationship with him/her. If a fee is refused, send a donation to the officiant's church or synagogue.

Tips To Save Money: Consider the officiant's fee when selecting your officiant and your ceremony site.

Price Range: $50 - $500

OFFICIANT'S GRATUITY

The officiant's gratuity is a discretionary amount of money given to the officiant for performing your wedding.

Things To Consider: This amount should depend on your relationship with the officiant and the amount of time s/he has spent with you prior to the ceremony. The groom puts this fee in a sealed envelope and gives it to his best man or wedding consultant, who gives it to the officiant either before or immediately after the ceremony.

Price Range: $25 - $250

GUEST BOOK / PEN / PENHOLDER

The guest book is a formal register where your guests sign-in as they arrive at the ceremony or reception. It serves as a memento of who attended your wedding. This book is often placed outside the ceremony or reception site, along with an elegant pen and penholder. A guest book attendant is responsible for inviting all guests to sign-in. A younger sibling or close friend who is not part of the wedding party may be well-suited for this position.

Options: There are many styles of guest books, pens and penholders to choose from. Some books have space for your guests to write a short note to the bride and groom.

Things To Consider: Make sure you have more than one pen in case one runs out of ink. If you are planning a large ceremony (over 300 guests), consider having more than one book and pen so that your guests don't have to wait in line to sign-in.

Price Range: $10 -$75

RING BEARER PILLOW

The ring bearer, usually a boy between the ages of four and eight, carries the bride and groom's rings or mock rings on a pillow. He follows the maid of honor and precedes the flower girl or bride in the processional.

Options: These pillows come in many styles and colors. You can find them at most gift shops and bridal boutiques.

Things To Consider: If the ring bearer is very young (less than 7 years), place mock rings on the pillow in place of the real rings to prevent losing them. If mock rings are used, instruct your ring bearer to put the pillow upside down during the recessional so your guests don't see the mock rings.

Tips To Save Money: Make your own ring bearer pillow by taking a small white pillow and attaching a pretty ribbon to it to hold the rings.

Price Range: $5 - $35

FLOWER GIRL BASKET

The flower girl, usually between the ages of four and eight, carries a basket filled with flowers, rose or paper rose petals to strew as she walks down the aisle. She follows the ring bearer or maid of honor and precedes the bride during the processional.

Options: Flower girl baskets come in many styles and colors. You can find them at most florists, gift shops, and bridal boutiques.

Things To Consider: Discuss any restrictions regarding rose petal, flower, or paper-tossing with your ceremony site. Select a basket which complements your guest book and ring bearer pillow. If the flower girl is very young (less than 7 years), consider giving her a small bouquet instead of a flower basket.

Tips To Save Money: Ask your florist if you can borrow a basket and attach a pretty white bow to it.

Price Range: $5 - $35

PERSONAL NOTES

WEDDING ATTIRE

BRIDAL GOWN

Bridal gowns come in a wide variety of styles, materials, colors, lengths and prices. You should order your gown at least four to six months before your wedding if your gown has to be ordered and then fitted.

Options: Different gown styles can help create a shorter, taller, heavier, or thinner look. Here are some tips:

* **A short, heavy figure:** To look taller and slimmer, avoid knit fabrics. Use the princess or A-line style. Chiffon is the best fabric choice because it produces a floating effect and camouflages weight.

* **A short, thin figure:** A shirtwaist or natural waist style with bouffant skirt will produce a taller, more rounded figure. Chiffon, velvet, lace and Schiffli net are probably the best fabric choices.

* **A tall, heavy figure:** Princess or A-line are the best styles for slimming the figure; satin, chiffon and lace fabrics are recommended.

● **A tall, thin figure:** Tiers or flounces will help reduce the impression of height. A shirtwaist or natural waist style with a full skirt are ideal choices. Satin and lace are the best fabrics.

The guidelines below will help you select the most appropriate gown for your wedding:

Informal wedding:	Street-length gown or suit Corsage or small bouquet No veil or train
Semi-formal wedding:	Floor-length gown Chapel train Finger-tip veil Small bouquet
Formal daytime wedding:	Floor-length gown Chapel or sweep train Fingertip veil or hat Gloves Medium-sized bouquet
Formal evening wedding:	Same as formal daytime except longer veil
Very formal wedding:	Floor-length gown Cathedral train Full-length veil Elaborate headpiece Long sleeves or long arm- covering gloves Cascading bouquet

Things To Consider: In selecting your bridal gown, keep in mind the time of year and formality of your wedding. It is a good idea to look at bridal magazines to compare the various styles and colors. If you see a gown you like, call boutiques in your area to see if they carry that line. Always try on the gown before ordering it.

When ordering a gown, make sure you order the correct size. If you are between sizes, order the larger one. You can always have your gown tailored down to fit, but it is not always possible to have it enlarged. Don't forget to ask when your gown will arrive, and be sure to get this in writing. The gown should arrive at least six weeks before the wedding so you can have it tailored and select the appropriate accessories to complement it.

Questions To Ask: The following questions may help you select a source for your bridal gown:

- What are your hours of operation?
- Are appointments needed?
- Do you offer any discounts or give-aways?
- What major bridal gown lines do you carry?
- Do you carry outfits for the mother of the bride?
- Do you carry bridesmaids gowns?
- Do you carry outfits for the flower girl and ring bearer?
- Do you rent tuxedos?
- What is the cost of the desired bridal gown?
- What is the cost of the desired headpiece?
- Do you offer in-house alterations? If so, what are your fees?
- Do you carry bridal shoes? What is their price range?

- Do you dye shoes to match outfits?
- Do you rent bridal slips? If so, what is the rental fee?
- What is the estimated date of delivery for my gown?
- What is your payment policy?
- What is your cancellation policy?

Beware: Some bridal boutiques have the practice of ordering gowns a size larger than needed. This requires more alterations which may mean extra charges. Ask for all alteration pricing in advance. Tailoring is a great source of income for boutiques. Also, gowns often fail to arrive on time, creating unnecessary stress for you. Have the store manager state, in writing, when the gown will arrive. And be sure to check the reputation of the boutique before buying.

Tips To Save Money: Consider renting a gown or buying one secondhand. Renting a gown usually costs about forty to sixty percent of its retail price. Consider this practical option if you are not planning to preserve the gown. The disadvantage of renting, however, is that your options are more limited. Also, a rented gown usually does not fit as well as a custom tailored gown.

Ask about discontinued styles and gowns. Watch for clearances and sales, or buy your gown "off the rack."

Restore or refurbish a family heirloom gown. If you have a friend, sister, or other family member who is planning a wedding, consider purchasing a gown that you could both wear. Change the veil and headpiece to personalize it.

Price Range: $300 - 3,000

ALTERATIONS

Alterations may be necessary in order to make your gown fit perfectly and conform smoothly to your body.

Things To Consider: Alterations usually require several fittings.   Allow four to six weeks for alterations to be completed. However, do not alter your gown months before the wedding. Your weight may fluctuate during the final weeks of planning and the gown might not fit properly.   Alterations are usually not included in the cost of the gown.

You may also want to consider making some modifications to your gown such as shortening or lengthening the train, customizing the sleeves, beading and so forth. Ask your bridal boutique what they charge for the modifications you are considering.

Tips To Save Money: Consider hiring an independent tailor. Their fees are usually lower than bridal boutiques.

Price Range: $50 - $150

HEADPIECE & VEIL

The headpiece is the part of the bride's outfit to which the veil is attached.

Options for Headpieces: Banana Clip, Bow, Garden Hat, Headband, Juliet Cap, Mantilla, Pillbox, Pouf, Snood, Tiara.

Options for Veils: Ballet, Bird Cage, Blusher, Cathedral Length, Chapel Length, Fingertip, Flyaway.

Things To Consider: The headpiece should complement but not overshadow your gown. In addition to the headpiece, you might want a veil. Veils come in different styles and lengths. Select a length which complements the length of your train. Consider the total look you're trying to achieve with your gown, headpiece, veil, and hairstyle.

Tips To Save Money: Some boutiques offer a free headpiece or veil with the purchase of a gown. Make sure you ask for this before purchasing your gown.

Price Range: $60 - $250

GLOVES

Gloves add a nice touch with either short-sleeved, three-quarter length, or sleeveless gowns.

Options: Gloves come in various styles and lengths. Depending on the length of your sleeves, select gloves that reach above your elbow, just below your elbow, halfway between your wrist and elbow, or only to your wrist. Fingerless mitts are another option that you may want to consider.

Things To Consider: You may want to consider fingerless mitts which allow the groom to place the wedding ring on your ring finger without having to remove your glove. You should not wear gloves if your gown has long sleeves, or if you're planning a small, at-home wedding.

Price Range: $5 - $30

JEWELRY

You will need to decide what jewelry to wear on your wedding day: earrings, necklace, bracelet and/or rings.

Options: Select pieces of jewelry that can be classified as "something old, something new, something borrowed, or something blue" (see page 184)

Things To Consider: Brides look best with just a few pieces of jewelry -- perhaps a string of pearls and earrings. You certainly don't want to draw attention away from your lovely gown.

Price Range: $60 - $1,000

STOCKINGS

Stockings should be selected with care, especially if the groom will be removing a garter from your leg at the reception.

Things To Consider: Consider having your maid of honor carry an extra pair, just in case you get a run.

Price Range: $5 - $15

GARTER

It is customary for the bride to wear a garter just above or below the knee on her wedding day. After the bouquet tossing ceremony, the groom takes the garter off the bride's leg. All the single men gather on the dance floor. The groom then tosses the garter to them over his back. According to age-old tradition, whoever catches the garter is the next to be married!

Things To Consider: You will need to choose the proper music for this event. A popular and fun song to play during the garter removal ceremony is *The Stripper,* by David Rose.

Price Range: $5 - $15

SHOES

Things To Consider: Make sure you select comfortable shoes that complement your gown; and don't forget to break them in well before your wedding day. Tight shoes can make you miserable and ruin your wedding day!

Price Range: $25 -$100

HAIRDRESSER

Many brides prefer to have their hair professionally arranged with their headpiece the day of the wedding rather than trying to do it themselves.

Things To Consider: If you decide to use a professional hairdresser the day of your wedding, be sure to have him/her experiment with your hair and headpiece before your wedding day so that there are no surprises. On your wedding day, you can either go to the salon or have the stylist meet you at your home or dressing site. Consider having him/her arrange your mother's and your bridesmaids' hair for a consistent look.

Tips To Save Money: Try to negotiate having your hair arranged free of charge or at a discount in exchange for bringing your mother, your fiancé's mother and your wedding party to the salon.

Price Range: $20 - $75 per person

MAKEUP ARTIST

Many brides prefer to have their makeup professionally applied on their wedding day rather than trying to do it themselves.

Things To Consider: It's smart to go for a trial run before the day of the wedding so that there are no surprises. You can either go to the salon or have the makeup artist meet you at your home or dressing site. Consider having him/her apply makeup for your mother, your fiancé's mother and your bridesmaids for a consistent look. In selecting a makeup artist, make sure s/he has been trained in makeup for photography. It is very important to wear the proper amount of makeup for photographs.

Tips To Save Money: Try to negotiate having your makeup applied free of charge or at a discount in exchange for bringing your mother, your fiancé's mother and your wedding party to the salon.

Price Range: $15 - $75 per person

MANICURE / PEDICURE

As a final touch, it's nice to have a professional manicure and/or pedicure the day of your wedding.

Things To Consider: Don't forget to bring the appropriate color nail polish with you for your appointment. You can either go to the salon or have the manicurist meet you at your home or dressing site. Consider having him/her give your mother, your fiancé's mother and your bridesmaids a manicure in the same color for a consistent look.

Tips To Save Money: Try to negotiate getting a manicure or pedicure free of charge or at a discount in exchange for bringing your mother, your fiancé's mother and your wedding party to the salon.

Price Range: $10 - $30 per person

GROOM'S FORMAL WEAR

The groom should select his formal wear based on the formality of the wedding. For a semi-formal or formal wedding, the groom will need a tuxedo. A tuxedo is the formal jacket worn by men on special or formal occasions. Popular colors are black, white, and gray.

Options: Use the following guidelines to select customary attire for the groom:

Informal wedding: Business suit
White dress shirt and tie

Semi-formal daytime: Formal suit
White dress shirt
Cummerbund or vest
Four-in-hand or bow tie

Semi-formal evening: Formal suit or dinner jacket
Matching trousers
White shirt
Cummerbund or vest
Black bow tie
Cufflinks and studs

Formal daytime: Cutaway or stroller jacket
Waistcoat
Striped trousers
White wing-collared shirt
Striped tie
Studs and cufflinks

Formal evening:

Black dinner jacket
Matching trousers
Waistcoat
White tuxedo shirt
Bow tie
Cummerbund or vest
Cufflinks

Very formal daytime:

Cutaway coat
Wing-collared shirt
Ascot
Striped trousers
Cufflinks
Gloves

Very formal evening:

Black tailcoat
Matching striped trousers
Bow tie
White wing-collared shirt
Waistcoat
Patent leather shoes
Studs and cufflinks
Gloves

Things To Consider: In selecting your formal wear, keep in mind the formality of your wedding, the time of day, and the bride's gown. Consider darker colors for a fall or winter wedding and lighter colors for a spring or summer wedding. When selecting a place to rent your tuxedo, check the reputation of the shop. Make sure they have a wide variety of makes and styles to choose from.

Reserve tuxedos for yourself and your ushers several weeks before the wedding to insure a wide selection and to allow enough time for alterations. Plan to pick up the tuxedos a few days before the wedding to allow time for last minute alterations in case they don't fit properly. Out-of-town men in your wedding party can be sized at any tuxedo shop. They can send their measurements to you or directly to the shop where you are going to rent your tuxedos.

Ask about the store's return policy and be sure you delegate to the appropriate person (usually your best man) the responsibility of returning all tuxedos within the time allotted. Ushers customarily pay for their own tuxedos.

Tips To Save Money: Try to negotiate getting your tuxedo for free or at a discount in exchange for having your father, your fiancé's father and ushers rent their tuxedos at that shop.

Price Range: $60 - $120

Personal Notes

*P*HOTOGRAPHY

BRIDE & GROOM'S ALBUM

The bride and groom's photo album is the best way to preserve your special day. Chances are you and your fiancé will look at the photos many times during your lifetime. Therefore, hiring a good photographer is one of the most important tasks in planning your wedding.

Options: There are a large variety of wedding albums. They vary in size, color, material, construction and price. Find one that you like and will feel proud of showing to your friends and family. Some of the most popular manufacturers of wedding albums are Art Leather, Leather Craftsman and Renaissance.

Make sure you review the differences between these albums before selecting one. You will also need to select the finish process of your photos. Ask your photographer to show you samples of various finishes. Some of the most popular finishes are glossy, lustre, semi-matte, pebble finish, spray texture and oil.

Things To Consider: Make sure you hire a photographer who specializes in weddings. Your photographer should be experienced in wedding procedures and familiar with your ceremony and reception sites. This will allow him/her to anticipate your next move and be in the proper place at the right time to capture all the special moments. Personal rapport is extremely important. The photographer may be an expert, but if you don't feel comfortable or at ease with him or her, your photography will reflect this. Comfort and compatibility with your photographer can make or break your wedding day and your photographs!

Look at his/her work. See if the photographer captured the excitement and emotion of the bridal couple. Also, remember that the wedding album should unfold like a story book -- the story of your wedding. Be sure to discuss with your photographer the photos you want so that there is no misunderstanding. A good wedding photographer should have a list of suggested poses to choose from. Some of the more popular poses are:

A)　Pre-Ceremony Photos:

>Wedding rings with the invitation.
>Bride getting dressed for the ceremony.
>Bride looking at her bridal bouquet.
>Maid of honor putting garter on bride's leg.
>Groom and best man before ceremony.
>Bride with her parents.
>Bride with her entire family and/or any
>　combination thereof.
>Bride with her bridesmaids.
>Bride with the flower girl and/or ring bearer.
>Groom with his parents.

Groom with his entire family and/or any
  combination thereof.
Groom with his ushers.
Groom with the bride's father.
Bride and her father, before walking down the
  aisle.

B)   **Ceremony Photos:**

Bride and groom saying their vows.
Bride and groom exchanging rings.
Groom kissing the bride at the altar.
Newlyweds with both of their families.
Newlyweds with the entire wedding party.
Bride and groom signing the marriage certificate.
Musicians.
Receiving Line.

C)   **Reception Photos:**

Grand entrance of newlyweds and their wedding
  party into the reception site.
Cake table.
Toasts.
First dance.
Cake-cutting ceremony.
Bouquet-tossing ceremony.
Garter-tossing ceremony.
Newlyweds leaving the reception for their
  honeymoon.
Candid shots of your guests.

Look at albums ready to be delivered, or proofs of weddings recently photographed. Look at the photographer's preferred style. Some photographers are known for formal poses, while others specialize in more candid, creative shots. Some can do both.

When asked to provide references, many photographers will give you the names of people they know are happy with their work. Some may even give you names from weddings they performed several years ago. This may not indicate the photographer's current ability or reputation. So when asking for references, be sure to ask for recent weddings the photographer has performed. This will give you a good idea of his/her current work. Be sure to ask if the photographer was prompt, cordial, properly dressed and whether s/he performed his/her duties as expected.

When comparing prices, consider the number, size and finish of the photographs and the type of album the photographer will use. Ask how many proofs you will get to choose your photos from. The more proofs, the better the selection you will have. Some photographers do not work with proofs. Rather, they simply supply you with a finished album after the wedding. Doing this may reduce the cost of your album but will also reduce your selection of photographs.

Questions To Ask: Make sure you ask all the following questions to ensure a smart hiring decision:

♦ How many years of experience do you have as a professional wedding photographer?

- What percentage of your total photography business is dedicated to weddings?
- Approximately how many weddings have you photographed?
- Are you the person who will photograph my wedding?
- Will you bring an assistant with you to my wedding?
- How do you typically dress for weddings?
- Do you have a professional studio?
- What type of equipment do you use?
- Do you bring backup equipment with you to weddings?
- Do you visit the ceremony and reception sites prior to the wedding?
- Do you have liability insurance?
- Are you skilled in diffused lighting & soft focus?
- Can you take studio portraits?
- Can you retouch negatives?
- Can negatives be purchased? If so, what is the cost?
- What is the cost of the package I am interested in?
- What does the desired package include?
- What is your payment policy?
- What is your cancellation policy?
- Do you offer a money-back guarantee?
- Do you use proofs?
- How many proofs will I get?
- When will I get my proofs?
- When will I get my album?
- What is the cost of an engagement portrait?
- What is the cost of a parent album?
- What is the cost of a 5" x 7" reprint?
- What is the cost of an 8" x 10" reprint?
- What is the cost of an 11" x 14" reprint?

- What is the cost per additional hour of shooting at the wedding?

Beware: Make sure the photographer you interview is the one who will photograph your wedding. There are many companies with more than one photographer. Often these companies use the work of the best photographer to sell their packages and then send a less experienced photographer to the wedding. Don't get caught in this trap! Be sure you meet with the photographer who will shoot your wedding. This way you can get an idea of his/her style and personality.

Also, some churches do not allow photographs to be shot during the ceremony. Make sure your photographer understands the rules and regulations of your church before planning the ceremony shots.

Tips To Save Money: Consider hiring a professional photographer for the formal shots of your ceremony only. You can then place disposable cameras on each table at the reception and let your guests take candid shots. This can save you a considerable amount of money in photography.

You can also lower the price of your album by paying for the photographs and then putting them into the album yourself. This is a very time-consuming task, so your photographer may reduce the price of his/her package if you opt to do this. To really economize, select a photographer who charges a flat fee to shoot the wedding and will allow you to purchase the film.

Compare at least 3 photographers for quality, value and price. Photographers who shoot weddings "on the side" are usually less expensive than professional wedding photographers.

Select a few 8" x 10"s for your album and more 4" x 5"s, and choose a moderately priced album.   Ask for specials and package deals.

Price Range: $400 - $3000

PARENTS' ALBUM

The parents' album is a smaller version of the bride and groom's album. It usually contains about twenty 5" x 7" photographs. Photos should be carefully selected for each individual family. If given as a gift, the album can be personalized with the bride and groom's names and date of the wedding on the front cover.

Tips To Save Money: Try to negotiate at least one free parents' album with the purchase of the bride and groom's album.

Price Range: $60 - $300

EXTRA PRINTS

Extra prints are photographs ordered in addition to the main album or parents' album.   These are usually purchased as gifts for the bridal party, close friends and family members.

Things To Consider: It is important to discuss the cost of extra prints since prices vary considerably. Some photographers offer the main album at great bargains to get the job, but then charge a fortune on extra prints. Think how many extra prints you would like to order and figure this into your budget before selecting your photographer.

Tips To Save Money: Ask your photographer to sell you the negatives. It's always less expensive to have the negatives developed into prints yourself than to order them from a professional photographer.

If you can wait, consider not ordering any reprints during the first few years after the wedding. A few years later, contact the photographer and ask if s/he will sell you the negatives. Most photographers will be glad to sell them at a bargain price. You can then make as many prints as you wish for a fraction of the cost.

Price Range: (5" x 7") = $3 - $15;   (8" x 10") = $10 - $25;   (11" x 14") = $25 - $75

PROOFS / PREVIEWS

Proofs/previews are the preliminary prints from which the bride and groom select photographs for their album and for their parents' albums. They are normally 5" x 5" in size.

Things To Consider: When selecting a package, ask how many proofs the photographer will take. The more proofs, the wider the selection you will have to choose from. For a wide selection, the photographer must take at least 2 to 3 times the number of prints that will go into your album.

Ask the photographer how soon after the wedding you will get your proofs. Request this in writing. The proofs should be ready by the time you get back from your honeymoon.   Also request to see your proofs before you make the final payment.

Tips To Save Money: Ask your photographer to use your proofs as part of your album package to save developing costs.

Price Range: $100 - $600

NEGATIVES

Negatives come in different sizes depending on the type of film and equipment used. The most popular camera for weddings is the medium format camera. When a medium format camera is used, the size of the negatives is 2 1/4" x 2 1/4."   When a 35 mm camera is used, the negatives are only 1" x 1 1/2." The larger the negative, the higher the quality of the photograph, especially when enlarged. Don't let a photographer convince you that there is no difference in quality between a 35 mm camera and a medium format camera.

Things To Consider: Most photographers will not sell you the negatives since they hope to make a profit on selling extra prints after the wedding. Ask the photographers you interview how long they keep the negatives. A professional photographer should keep the negatives at least five years. Make sure you get this in writing.

Tips To Save Money: Purchasing the negatives will save you a lot of money when duplicating prints for family and friends. But don't spend money on purchasing negatives unless you are planning to make a lot of reprints. If you can wait, consider not buying the negatives right away. Contact the photographer a few years later and ask if s/he will sell you the negatives. Most photographers will be glad to sell them at a bargain price.

Price Range: $100 - $800

ENGAGEMENT PHOTOGRAPH

The engagement photograph is sent to your local newspapers, along with information announcing your engagement to the public. This announcement is usually made by the bride's parents or her immediate family.

Things To Consider: The photograph (usually in black and white) was traditionally of the bride alone, but today is usually of the engaged couple.

Tips To Save Money: Look at engagement photographs in your local newspaper. Then have a friend or family member take a photograph of you and your fiancé in a pose similar to the ones you have seen.

Price Range: $35 - $75

FORMAL BRIDAL PORTRAIT

If you intend to announce your marriage in the newspaper the day after your wedding, you will need to have a formal bridal portrait taken several weeks before the wedding. This is a photograph of the bride taken before the wedding in the photographer's studio. This photograph, along with an announcement, must be sent to your local newspapers as soon as possible.

Things To Consider: Some fine bridal salons provide an attractive background where the bride may arrange to have her formal bridal photograph taken after the final fitting of her gown. This will save you the hassle of bringing your gown and headpiece to the photographer's studio and dressing up once again.

Tips To Save Money: If you don't mind announcing your marriage several weeks after the wedding, consider having your formal portrait taken the day of your wedding. This will save you the studio costs, the hassle of getting dressed for the photo, and the photograph will be more natural since the bridal bouquet will be the one you actually carried down the aisle. Also, brides are always most beautiful on their wedding day!

Price Range: $50 - $150

Personal Notes

VIDEOGRAPHY

MAIN VIDEO

Next to your photo album, videography is the best way to preserve your wedding memories. Unlike photographs, videography captures the mood of the wedding day in motion and sound. You have the option of selecting one, two, or three cameras. The more cameras used, the more action captured and the more expensive. An experienced videographer, however, can do a good job with just one camera.

Options: There are various types of video cameras available. Commercial cameras are the best. These are used for television and special events. The next best cameras are Super VHS followed by Super 8 mm. Compare videographer's equipment when comparing their packages and prices. And don't forget to ask if your videographer has a wireless microphone. It will come in handy during the ceremony when you want to capture all the words at a distance without the need for a long cable.

Things To Consider: Look at previous weddings the videographer has videotaped. Notice the color and brightness of the screen, as well as the quality of the sound. This will indicate the quality of his/her equipment. Notice the picture -- is it smooth or jerky? This will indicate the videographer's level of skill. Notice any special effects such as titles, dissolve, and multiple screens.

Make sure you hire someone who specializes in weddings. Just like your photographer, your videographer should be experienced in wedding procedures and, ideally, should be familiar with the layout of your ceremony and reception sites. This will allow him/her to anticipate your next move and be in the proper place at the right time to capture all the special moments.

Remember to ask your videographer to interview your wedding party, close friends and family members, asking them to make a wish or toast to both of you as a married couple, or to tell any "wild" stories they may want to share for the record. This personalizes your video and is a wonderful memento. Consider both personality and professionalism when hiring your videographer.

Find out what is included in each package you are considering: hours of coverage, titling, in-camera editing or post-editing. If you will be getting married in a church, find out the church's policies regarding videography. Some churches do not allow a videographer to be close to the ceremony.

To preserve your wedding video for years to come, store it in a cool, dark place away from dust and dirt.

Questions To Ask: Make sure you ask all the following questions to ensure a smart hiring decision:

- How many years of experience do you have as a professional wedding videographer?
- Approximately how many weddings have you taped?
- Are you the person who will videotape my wedding?
- Will you bring an assistant with you to my wedding?
- How do you dress for weddings?
- Do you have professional editing equipment?
- What type of equipment do you use?
- Do you have a wireless microphone?
- Can you videotape in low light?
- What format do you use (VHS, Super VHS, 8mm)?
- Do you bring backup equipment with you?
- Do you visit the ceremony and reception sites before the wedding?
- Do you edit the tape after the event?
- Who keeps the raw footage?
- When will I receive the final product?
- Can you make a photo montage? If so, at what price?
- What is the cost of the package I am interested in?
- What does the desired package include?
- What is your payment policy?
- What is your cancellation policy?
- Do you offer a money-back guarantee?

Beware: As in photography, there are many companies with more than one videographer. These companies often use the work of the best videographer to sell their packages and then send a less experienced videographer to the wedding. Again, don't get caught in this trap! Be sure to interview the videographer who will shoot your wedding so you can get a good idea of his/her style and personality. Ask to see his/her own work.

Tips To Save Money: Compare videographers' quality, value and price. There is a wide range, and the most expensive is not necessarily the best. One camera is the most cost effective and may be all you need. Consider hiring a company that offers both videography and photography. You may save overall.

Ask a family member or close friend to videotape your wedding. However, realize that without professional equipment and expertise the final product may not be quite the same.

Price Range: $350 - $2,000

TITLES

Titles and subtitles can be edited into your video before or after the filming. Titles are important since twenty years from now you might not remember the exact time of your wedding or the names of your wedding party members. Some videographers charge more for titling. Make sure you discuss this with your videographer and get in writing exactly what titles will be included.

Options: Titles may include the date, time and location of the wedding, the bride and groom's names, and names of special family members and/or the wedding party. Titles may also include special thanks to those who helped with the wedding. You can send these people a copy of your video after the wedding. This is a very appropriate and inexpensive gift!

Tips To Save Money: Consider borrowing a camera with a character generator from a friend and doing the titling yourself.

Price Range: $40 - $75

EXTRA HOURS

Find out how much your videographer would charge to stay longer than contracted for in your original package. If this is not disclosed, a videographer can charge a fortune if asked to stay longer. Don't forget to get this in writing.

Tips To Save Money: Avoid paying extra hours beyond what's included in your selected package. You can do this by calculating the number of hours you think you'll need and negotiating that into your package price. Consider taping the ceremony only. Eliminate the extras such as titles and photo montage. You can do this yourself.

Price Range: $35 - $60/hour

PHOTO MONTAGE

A photo montage is a series of photographs set to music on video. The number of photographs depends on the length of the song and the amount of time allotted for each photograph. A typical song usually allows for approximately 40 to 50 photographs. Photo montages are a great way to reproduce your photographs. Copies of this video can be made for considerably less than the cost of reproducing photographs.

Options: Photo montages can be made of you and your fiancé growing up, the rehearsal, the wedding day, the honeymoon, or any combination thereof.

Things To Consider: Send copies of your photo montage video to close friends and family members as mementos of your wedding.

Tips To Save Money: Consider making a photo montage yourself. This is very easily done with any video camera, a tripod, and a good stereo. The secret is in holding the camera very still and having the proper lighting while videotaping the photographs.

Price Range: $50 - $100

EXTRA COPIES

A professional videographer will be able to reproduce your video much easier and better than you can, provided s/he has professional equipment. Be sure to ask your videographer how much s/he charges for extra copies of the wedding videotape. You'll certainly want to give your parents a copy!

Tips To Save Money: Borrow a VCR from a friend and make copies yourself.

Price Range: $5 - $35

STATIONERY

INVITATIONS

Begin creating your guest list as soon as possible. Ask
your parents and the groom's parents for a list of the people they would like to invite. You and your fiancé should
make your own list. Make certain that all names are
spelled correctly and that all addresses are current. Determine if you wish to include children; if so, add their
names to your list. All children over the age of 16 should
receive their own invitation.

Order your invitations at least 4 months before the wedding. Allow an additional month for engraved invitations. Invitations are traditionally issued by the bride's
parents; but if the groom's parents are assuming some of
the wedding costs, the invitations should be in their
names also. Mail all invitations at the same time, 6 - 8
weeks before the wedding.

Options: There are three types of invitations:
traditional/formal, contemporary, and informal.   The
traditional/formal wedding invitation is white, soft cream,
or ivory with raised black lettering. The printing is done
on the top page of a double sheet of thick quality paper;
the inside is left blank. The contemporary invitation is

typically an individualized presentation that makes a statement about the bride and groom. Informal invitations are often printed on the front of a single, heavyweight card and may be handwritten or preprinted.

There are three types of printing: engraved, thermography, and offset printing. Engraving is the most expensive, traditional and formal type of printing. It also takes the longest to complete. In engraved printing, stationery is pressed onto a copper plate, which makes the letters rise slightly from the page. Thermography is a process that fuses powder and ink to create a raised letter. This takes less time than engraving and is less expensive because copper plates do not have to be engraved. Offset printing, the least expensive, is the quickest to produce and offers a variety of styles and colors. It is also the least formal.

Things To Consider: If all your guests are to be invited to both the ceremony and the reception, a combined invitation may be sent without separate enclosure cards. Order one invitation for each married or cohabiting couple that you plan to invite. The officiant and his/her spouse as well as your attendants should receive an invitation.

Order approximately 20% more stationery than your actual head count. Allow a minimum of two weeks to address and mail the invitations, longer if using a calligrapher or if your guest list is very large. You may also want to consider ordering invitations to the rehearsal dinner, as these should be in the same style as the wedding invitation.

SAMPLES OF TRADITIONAL/FORMAL INVITATIONS

1)   **When the bride's parents sponsor the wedding:**

Mr. and Mrs. Alexander Waterman Smith
request the honor of your presence
at the marriage of their daughter
Carol Ann
to
Mr. William James Clark
on Saturday, the fifth of August
Nineteen hundred and ninety-four
at two o'clock in the afternoon
Saint James by-the-Sea
La Jolla, California

2)   **When the groom's parents sponsor the wedding:**

Mr. and Mrs. Michael Burdell Clark
request the honor of your presence
at the marriage of
Miss Carol Ann Smith
to their son
Mr. William James Clark

3)   When both the bride and groom's parents sponsor the wedding:

Mr. and Mrs. Alexander Waterman Smith
and
Mr. and Mrs. Michael Burdell Clark
request the honor of your presence
at the marriage of their children
Miss Carol Ann Smith
to
Mr. William James Clark

OR

Mr. and Mrs. Alexander Waterman Smith
request the honor of your presence
at the marriage of their daughter
Carol Ann Smith
to
William James Clark
son of Mr. and Mrs. Michael Burdell Clark

4)   When the bride and groom sponsor their own wedding:

The honor of your presence is requested
at the marriage of
Miss Carol Ann Smith
and
Mr. William James Clark

OR
Miss Carol Ann Smith
and
Mr. William James Clark
request the honor of your presence
at their marriage

5)   With divorced or deceased parents:

When the bride's mother is sponsoring the wedding and is
not remarried:

Mrs. Julie Hurden Smith
requests the honor of your presence
at the marriage of her daughter
Carol Ann

When the bride's mother is sponsoring and has remarried:

Mrs. Julie Hurden Booker
requests the honor of your presence
at the marriage of her daughter
Carol Ann Smith

OR

Mr. and Mrs. John Thomas Booker
request the honor of your presence
at the marriage of Mrs. Booker's daughter
Carol Ann Smith

When the bride's father is sponsoring the wedding and has not remarried:

Mr. Alexander Waterman Smith
requests the honor of your presence
at the marriage of his daughter
Carol Ann

When the bride's father is sponsoring and has remarried:

Mr. and Mrs. Alexander Waterman Smith
request the honor of your presence
at the marriage of Mr. Smith's daughter
Carol Ann

6)   Deceased parents:

Both parents are deceased and a close friend or relative sponsors the wedding:

Mr. and Mrs. Brandt Elliott Lawson
request the honor of your presence
at the marriage of their granddaughter
Carol Ann Smith

7)   In military ceremonies, the rank determines the placement of names:

Any title lower than sergeant should be omitted. Only the branch of service should be included under that person's name:

Mr. and Mrs. Alexander Waterman Smith
request the honor of your presence
at the marriage of their daughter
Carol Ann
United States Army
to
William James Clark

Junior officers' titles are placed below their names **and are**
followed by their branch of service:

Mr. and Mrs. Alexander Waterman Smith
request the honor of your presence
at the marriage of their daughter
Carol Ann
to
William James Clark
First Lieutenant, United States Army

If the rank is higher than lieutenant, titles **are placed be-**
fore names, and the branch of service is placed on **the fol-**
lowing line:

Mr. and Mrs. Alexander Waterman Smith
request the honor of your presence
at the marriage of their daughter
Carol Ann
to
Captain William James Clark
United States Navy

SAMPLE OF A LESS FORMAL,
MORE CONTEMPORARY INVITATION

Mr. and Mrs. Alexander Waterman Smith
would like you to
join with their daughter
Carol Ann
and
William James Clark
in the celebration of their marriage

Tips To Save Money: Thermography looks like engraving and is one-third the cost. Choose paper stock that is reasonable and yet achieves your overall look. Select invitations that can be mailed with a single stamp. Order at least 25 extra invitations, just in case you add people to your list or mess some up. To reorder this small number of invitations later would cost nearly three times the amount you'll spend up front.

Price Range: $0.75 - $5 per invitation

RESPONSE CARDS

Response cards are enclosed with the invitation to determine the number of people who will be attending your wedding. They are the smallest card size accepted by the postal service and should be printed in the same style as the invitation. An invitation to only the wedding ceremony does not usually include a request for a reply. However, response cards should be used when it is necessary to have an exact head count for special seating arrangements. If included, these cards should be easy for your guests to understand and use. Include a self-addressed and stamped return envelope to make it easy for your guests to return the response cards.

Things To Consider: You should not include a line that reads "number of persons" on your response cards because only those whose names appear on the inner and outer envelopes are invited. Each couple, each single person, and all children over the age of 16 should receive their own invitation. Indicate on the inner envelope if they may bring an escort or guest. The omitting of children's names from the inner envelope infers that the children are not invited.

Samples of wording for response cards:

M_____

(The M may be eliminated from the line, especially if many Drs. are invited)

___ accepts

___ regrets

Saturday the fifth of July

Oceanside Country Club

OR

The favor of your reply is requested

by the twenty-second of May

M_____

will _____ attend

Price Range: $.40 - $.80 each

RECEPTION CARDS

If the guest list for the ceremony is larger than that for the reception, a separate card with the date, time and location for the reception should be enclosed with the ceremony invitation for those guests also invited to the reception. Reception cards should be placed in front of the invitation, facing the back flap and the person inserting them. They should be printed on the same quality paper and in the same style as the invitation itself.

Sample of a formally-worded reception card:

> Mr. and Mrs. Alexander Waterman Smith
> request the pleasure of your company
> Saturday, the third of July
> at three o'clock
> Oceanside Country Club
> 2020 Waterview Lane
> Oceanside, California

Sample of a less formal reception card:

> Reception immediately following the ceremony
> Oceanside Country Club
> 2020 Waterview Lane
> Oceanside, California

Things To Consider: You may also include a reception card in all your invitations if the reception is to be held at a different site than the ceremony.

Tips To Save Money: If all people invited to the ceremony are also invited to the reception, include the reception information on the invitation and eliminate the reception card. This will save printing and postage costs.

Price Range: $.35 - $.60 each

CEREMONY CARDS

If the guest list for the reception is larger than the guest list for the ceremony, a special insertion card with the date, time and location for the ceremony should be enclosed with the reception invitation for those guests also invited to the ceremony.

Ceremony cards should be placed in front of the invitation, facing the back flap and the person inserting them. They should be printed on the same quality paper and in the same style as the invitation itself.

Price Range: $.35 - $.60 each

PEW CARDS

Pew cards may be used to let special guests and family members know they are to be seated in the reserved section on either the bride's side or the groom's side. These are most typically seen in large, formal ceremonies. Guests should take this card to the ceremony and show it to the ushers, who should then escort them to their seats.

Options: Pew cards may indicate a specific pew number if specific seats are assigned, or may read "Within the Ribbon" if a certain number of pews are reserved but no specific seat is assigned.

Things To Consider: Pew cards may be inserted along with the invitation, or may be sent separately after the RSVPs have been returned. It is often easier to send them after you have received all RSVPs so you know how many reserved pews will be needed.

Tips To Save Money: Include the pew card with the invitation and just say "Within the Ribbon." After you have received all your RSVPs, you will know how many pews will need to be reserved for these special guests. This will save you the cost of mailing the pew cards separately.

Price Range: $.20 - $.60 each

SEATING / PLACE CARDS

Seating/place cards are used to let guests know where they should be seated at the reception and are a good way of putting people together so they feel most comfortable. Place cards should be laid out alphabetically on a table at the entrance to the reception. Each card should correspond to a table -- either by number, color, or other identifying factor. Each table should be marked accordingly.

Options: Select a traditional or contemporary design for your place cards, depending on the style of your wedding.

Regardless of the design, place cards must contain the same information: the bride and groom's names on the first line; the date on the second line; the third line is left blank for you to write in the guest's name; and the fourth line is for the table number, color, or other identifying factor.

Price Range: $.20 - $.60 each

RAIN CARDS

These cards are enclosed when guests are invited to an outdoor ceremony and/or reception, informing them of an alternate location in case of bad weather. As with other enclosures, rain cards should be placed in front of the invitation, facing the back flap and the person inserting them. They should be printed on the same quality paper and in the same style as the invitation itself.

Price Range: $.20 - $.30 each

MAPS

Maps to the ceremony and/or reception are becoming frequent inserts in wedding invitations. They need to be drawn and printed in the same style as the invitation and are usually on a small, heavier card. If they are not printed in the same style or on the same type of paper as the invitation, they should be mailed separately.

Options: Maps should include both written and visual instructions, keeping in mind the fact that guests may be coming from different locations.

Things To Consider: Order extra maps to hand out at the ceremony if the reception is at a different location.

Tips To Save Money: If you are comfortable with computers, you can purchase software that allows you to draw your own maps. Print a map to both the ceremony and reception on the same sheet of paper, perhaps one on each side. This will save you the cost of mailing two maps. Or have your ushers hand out maps to the reception after the ceremony.

Price Range: $.50 - $.75 each

CEREMONY PROGRAMS

Ceremony programs are printed documents showing the sequence of events during the ceremony. These programs add a personal touch to your wedding and are a convenient way of letting guests know who your attendants, officiant, and ceremony musicians are. For example:

The Marriage of
Carol Ann Smith and William James Clark
the fourth of March, 2000
San Diego, California

Our Ceremony

Prelude:
All I Ask of You, by Andrew Lloyd Webber

Processional:
The Canon, by Pachelbel

Rite of Marriage

Welcome guests

Statement of intentions

Marriage vows

Exchange of rings

Blessing of bride and groom

Pronouncement of marriage

Presentation of the bride and groom

Recessional:
Trumpet Voluntary, by Jeromiah Clarke

Our Wedding Party

Maid of Honor:
Susan Smith, Sister of Bride

Best Man:
Brandt Clark, Brother of Groom

Bridesmaids:
Janet Anderson, Friend of Bride
Lisa Bennett, Friend of Bride

Ushers:
Mark Gleason, Friend of Groom
Tommy Olson, Friend of Groom

Officiant:
Father Henry Thomas

Our Reception

Please join us after the ceremony
in the celebration of our marriage at:
La Valencia Hotel
1132 Prospect Street
La Jolla, CA

Options: Ceremony programs can be handed out to guests by the ushers, or they can be placed at the back of the church for guests to take as they enter.

Price Range: $.75 - $1.75 each

ANNOUNCEMENTS

Announcements are not obligatory but do serve a useful purpose. They may be sent to those friends who are not invited to the wedding because the number of guests must be limited, or because they live too far away. They may also be sent to acquaintances who, while not particularly close to the family, might still wish to know of the marriage.

Announcements are also appropriate for friends and acquaintances who are not expected to attend and for whom you do not want to give an obligation of sending a gift. They should include the day, month, year, city, and state where the ceremony took place.

Things To Consider: Announcements should never be sent to anyone who has received an invitation to the ceremony or the reception. They are printed on the same paper and in the same style as the invitations. They should be addressed before the wedding and mailed the day of or the day after the ceremony.

Price Range: $.50 - $1

THANK-YOU NOTES

Regardless of whether the bride has thanked the donor in person or not, she must write a thank-you note for every gift received.

Things To Consider: Order thank-you notes along with your other stationery at least four months before your wedding. You should order some with your maiden initials for thank-you notes sent before the ceremony, and the rest with your married initials for notes sent after the wedding and for future use. Send thank-you notes within two weeks of receiving a gift that arrives before the wedding, and within two months after the honeymoon for gifts received on or after your wedding day. Be sure to mention the gift you received in the body of the note and let the person know how much you like it and what you and your spouse plan to do with it.

Price Range: $.30 - $.50

STAMPS

Don't forget to budget stamps for response cards as well as for invitations!

Things To Consider: Don't order your stamps until you have had the post office weigh your completed invitation. It may exceed the size and weight for one stamp. Order commemorative stamps that fit the occasion.

Price Range: $.33 - $1

CALLIGRAPHY

Calligraphy is a form of elegant handwriting often used to address invitations for formal occasions. Traditional wedding invitations should be addressed by hand in black or blue fountain pen.

Options: You may address the invitations yourself, hire a professional calligrapher, or have your invitations addressed using calligraphy by computer. Make sure you use the same method or person to address both the inner and outer envelopes.

Tips To Save Money: You may want to consider taking a short course to learn the art of calligraphy so that you can address your own invitations. If you have a computer with a laser printer, you can also address the invitations yourself using calligraphy fonts. There are many beautiful styles to choose from.

Price Range: $.30 - $3 each

NAPKINS AND MATCHBOOKS

Napkins and matchbooks may also be ordered from your stationer. These are placed around the reception room as decorative items and mementos of the event.

Things To Consider: Napkins and matchbooks can be printed in your wedding colors or white with gold or silver lettering. Include both of your names and the wedding date. You may consider including a phrase or thought, or a small graphic design above your names.

Price Range: $.5 - $1.50 each

Personal Notes

*A*DDRESSING *E*NVELOPES

Use the following guidelines for addressing invitations:

Husband and Wife (with same surname)

> **Inner Envelope**
> Mr. and Mrs. Smith
>
> **Outer Envelope**
> Mr. and Mrs. Thomas Smith
> (use middle name, if known)

Husband and Wife (with different surnames)

> **Inner Envelope**
> Ms. Banks and Mr. Smith
> (wife first)
>
> **Outer Envelope**
> Ms. Angela Banks
> Mr. Thomas Smith
> (wife's name above husband's)

Husband and Wife (wife has professional title)

Inner Envelope
Dr. Smith and Mr. Smith

Outer Envelope
Dr. Anita Smith
Mr. Thomas Smith
(wife's name & title above husband's)

Husband and Wife With Children under 16

Inner Envelope
Mr. and Mrs. Smith
John, Mary, and Glen
(in order of age)

Outer Envelope
Mr. and Mrs. Thomas Smith

Single Woman (regardless of age)

Inner Envelope
Miss/Ms. Smith

Outer Envelope
Miss/Ms. Beverly Smith

Single Woman and Guest

> **Inner Envelope**
> Miss/Ms. Smith
> Mr. Jones (or "and Guest")
>
> **Outer Envelope**
> Miss/Ms. Beverly Smith

Single Man

> **Inner Envelope**
> Mr. Jones
> (Master for a young boy)
>
> **Outer Envelope**
> Mr. William Jones

Single Man and Guest

> **Inner Envelope**
> Mr. Jones
> Miss/Ms. Smith (or "and Guest")
>
> **Outer Envelope**
> Mr. William Jones

Unmarried Couple Living Together

Inner Envelope
Mr. Knight and Ms. Orlandi
(names listed alphabetically)

Outer Envelope
Mr. Michael Knight
Ms. Paula Orlandi

Two Sisters (over 16)

Inner Envelope
The Misses Smith

Outer Envelope
The Misses Mary and Jane Smith
(in order of age)

Two Brothers (over 16)

Inner Envelope
The Messrs. Smith

Outer Envelope
The Messrs. John and Glen Smith
(in order of age)

<u>Brothers & Sisters (over 16)</u>

> **Inner Envelope**
> Mary, Jane, John & Glen
> (name the girls first, in order of age)

> **Outer Envelope**
> The Misses Smith
> The Messrs. Smith
> (name the girls first)

<u>A Brother and Sister (over 16)</u>

> **Inner Envelope**
> Jane and John
> (name the girl first)

> **Outer Envelope**
> Miss Jane Smith and Mr. John Smith
> (name the girl first)

<u>Widow</u>

> **Inner Envelope**
> Mrs. Smith

> **Outer Envelope**
> Mrs. William Smith

Divorcee

Inner Envelope
Mrs. Smith

Outer Envelope
Mrs. Jones Smith
(maiden name and former husband's
surname)

*R*ECEPTION

RECEPTION SITE FEE

The reception is a party where all your guests come together to celebrate your new life as a married couple. It should reflect and complement the formality of your ceremony. The selection of a reception site will depend on its availability, price, proximity to the ceremony site, and the number of people it will accommodate.

There are two basic types of reception sites. The first type charges a per person fee which includes the facility, food, tables, silverware, china, and so forth. Examples: hotels, restaurants and catered yachts. The second type charges a room rental fee and you are responsible for providing the food, beverages, linens, and possibly tables and chairs. Examples: clubs, halls, parks, museums, and private homes.

The advantage of the first type is that most everything is done for you. The disadvantage, however, is that your choices of food, china, and linen are limited. Usually you are not permitted to bring in an outside caterer and must select from a predetermined menu.

Options: Private homes, gardens, hotels, clubs, restaurants, halls, parks, museums, yachts, and wineries are some of the more popular choices for receptions.

Things To Consider: When comparing the cost of different locations, consider the rental fee, food, beverages, parking, gratuity, set-up charges and the cost of rental equipment needed such as tables, chairs, canopies, and so forth. If you are planning an outdoor reception, be sure to have a backup site in case of rain.

Questions To Ask: Make sure you ask all the following questions before selecting a reception site:

- What is the name & phone number of my contact person?
- What dates & times are available?
- What is the maximum number of guests for a seated reception?
- What is the maximum number of guests for a cocktail reception?
- What is the reception site fee?
- What is the price range for a seated lunch?
- What is the price range for a buffet lunch?
- What is the price range for a seated dinner?
- What is the price range for a buffet dinner?
- Can we keep the left over food?
- What is the corkage fee?
- What is the cake-cutting fee?
- What is the ratio of servers to guests?
- How much time will be allotted for my reception?
- What music restrictions are there, if any?
- What alcohol restrictions are there, if any?

- Are there any restrictions for rice or rose petal-tossing?
- What room and table decorations are available?
- Is a changing room available?
- Is there handicap accessibility?
- Is a dance floor included in the site fee?
- Are tables, chairs, and linens included in the site fee?
- Are outside caterers allowed?
- Are kitchen facilities available for outside caterers?
- Does the facility have full liability insurance?
- What "perks" or giveaways are offered?
- How many parking spaces are available for my family and wedding party?
- How many parking spaces are available for my guests?
- What is the cost for parking, if any?
- What is the cost for sleeping rooms, if available?
- What is the payment policy?
- What is the cancellation policy?
- Are credit cards accepted?

Beware: Some hotels are known for double booking. A bride may reserve the largest or most elegant room in a hotel for her reception, only to find out later that the hotel took the liberty to book a more profitable event in the room she had reserved and moved her reception over to a smaller or less elegant room.

Also be careful of hotels that book events too close together. You don't want your guests to wait outside while your room is being set up for the reception. And you don't want to be "forced out" before you are ready to leave because the hotel needs to arrange the room for the next reception. Get your rental hours and the name of your room in writing.

Tips To Save Money: Since the cost of the reception is approximately 35% of the total cost of your wedding, you can save the most money by limiting your guest list. If you hire a wedding consultant, s/he may be able to cut your cake and save you the cake-cutting fee. Check this out with your facility or caterer. Reception sites that charge a room rental fee may waive this fee if you meet minimum requirements on food and beverages consumed. But try to negotiate this before you book the facility.

Price Range: $300 - $1,000

HORS D' OEUVRES

At receptions where a full meal is to be served, hors d' oeuvres may be offered to guests during the first hour of the reception. However, at a tea or cocktail reception, hors d' oeuvres will be the "main course."

Options: There are many options for hors d' oeuvres, depending on the formality of your reception and the type of food to be served at the meal. Popular items are foods that can easily be picked up and eaten with one hand. Hors d' oeuvres may be set out on tables "buffet style" for guests to help themselves, or they may be passed around on trays by waiters and waitresses.

Things To Consider: When selecting hors d' oeuvres for your reception, consider whether heating or refrigeration will be available and choose your food accordingly. When planning your menu, consider the time of day. You should select lighter hors d' oeuvres for a midday reception and heavier hors d' oeuvres for an evening reception.

Tips To Save Money: Tray pass hors d'oeuvres during cocktail hour and serve a lighter meal. Avoid serving hors d'oeuvres that are labor intensive or that require expensive ingredients. Compare two or three caterers; there is a wide price range between caterers for the same food. Compare the total cost of catering (main meal plus hors d'oeuvres) when selecting a caterer. Consider serving hors d'oeuvres "buffet style." Your guests will eat less this way than if waiters and waitresses are constantly serving them hors d'oeuvres.

Price Range: $1 - $10/person

MAIN MEAL / CATERER

If your reception is going to be in a hotel, restaurant or other facility that provides food, you will need to select a meal to serve your guests. Most of these facilities will have a predetermined menu from which to select your meal. If your reception is going to be in a facility that does not provide food, you will need to hire an outside caterer. The caterer will be responsible for preparing, cooking, decorating and serving the food.

The caterer will also be responsible for beverages and for cleaning up after the event. Before signing a contract, make sure you understand all the services the caterer will provide. Your contract should state the amount and type of food and beverages that will be served, the way in which they will be served, the number of servers who will be available, the cost per item or person, and the rental items the caterer will provide such as tables, chairs and tableware.

Options: Food can be served either buffet-style or as a sit-down meal. It should be chosen according to the time of day, year, and formality of the wedding. Although there are many main dishes to choose from, chicken and beef are the most popular selections for a large event. Ask your facility manager or caterer for their specialty. If you have a special type of food you would like to serve at your reception, select a facility or caterer who specializes in preparing it.

Things To Consider: When hiring a caterer, check to see if the location for your reception provides refrigeration and cooking equipment. If not, make sure your caterer is fully self supported with portable refrigeration and heating equipment. A competent caterer will prepare much of the food in his/her own kitchen and should provide an adequate staff of cooks, servers, and bartenders. Ask for references and look at photos from previous parties so you know how the food will be presented; or better yet, visit an event they are catering.

Questions To Ask: Be sure to ask all the following questions before selecting a caterer:
♦ What is the name and phone number of my contact person?

- How many years have you been in business?
- What percentage of your catering business is dedicated to wedding receptions?
- Do you have liability insurance?
- Are you licensed to serve alcohol?
- What is your ratio of servers to guests?
- How do your servers dress for wedding receptions?
- What is your price range for a seated lunch?
- What is your price range for a buffet lunch?
- What is your price range for a seated dinner?
- What is your price range for a buffet dinner?
- How much gratuity is expected?
- What is your labor fee per employee?
- What is your cake-cutting fee?
- What is your bartending fee?
- What is your fee to clean-up after the reception?
- What is your payment policy?
- What is your cancellation policy?
- Do you accept credit cards?
- When is the final head-count needed?

Beware: Avoid mayonnaise, cream sauces, or custard fillings if food must go unrefrigerated for any length of time.

Tips To Save Money: Give only 85 to 95 percent of your final guest count to your caterer or facility manager, depending on how certain you are that all of your guests who have responded will come. Chances are that several, if not many, of your guests will not show up. If they do, your caterer should have enough food for all of them. This is especially true with buffet style receptions, in which case the facility or caterer will charge extra for each additional guest. However, if you give a complete count of your guests to your caterer and some of them don't show up, you will still have to pay for their plates. If offering a buffet meal, have the catering staff serve the food onto guests' plates rather than allowing guests to serve themselves. This will help to regulate the amount of food consumed.

Select food that is not too time-consuming to prepare, or food that does not have expensive ingredients. Also, consider a brunch or early afternoon wedding so the reception will fall between meals, allowing you to serve hors d'oeuvres instead of a full meal. Or tray pass hors d'oeuvres during cocktail hour and choose a lighter meal.

Price Range:　$10 - $60/person

LIQUOR / BEVERAGES

Prices for liquor and beverages vary greatly, depending on the amount and brand of alcohol served. It is an expected tradition that at least champagne or punch be served to toast the couple.

Options:　White and red wines, scotch, vodka, gin, rum, and beer are the most popular alcoholic beverages. Sodas and fruit punch are popular nonalcoholic beverages served at receptions. And of course, don't forget coffee or tea. There are a number of options and variations for serving alcoholic beverages: a full open bar where you pay for your guests to drink as much as they wish; an open bar for the first hour, followed by a cash bar where guests pay for their own drinks; cash bar only; beer and wine only; nonalcoholic beverages only; or any combination thereof.

Things To Consider: If you're hosting an open bar at a facility that provides alcohol, ask the catering manager how they charge for liquor: by consumption or by number of bottles opened. Get this in writing and then ask for a full consumption report after the event.

If you plan to serve alcoholic beverages at a facility that does not provide liquor, make sure your caterer has a license to serve alcohol and that the facility allows alcoholic beverages. If you plan to order your own alcohol, do so three or four weeks before the event. If you plan to have a no-host or "cash" bar, consider notifying your guests so they know to bring cash with them. A simple line that says "No-Host Bar" on the reception card should suffice.

In selecting the type of alcohol to serve, consider the age and preference of your guests, the type of food that will be served, and the time of day your guests will be drinking.

On the average, you should allow 1 drink per person per hour at the reception. A bottle of champagne will usually serve six glasses. Never serve liquor without some type of food. Use the following chart to plan your beverage needs:

Beverages	Amount based on 100 guests
Bourbon	3 Fifths
Gin	3 Fifths
Rum	2 Fifths
Scotch	4 Quarts
Vodka	5 Quarts
White Wine	2 Cases
Red Wine	1 Case
Champagne	3 Cases
Other	2 Cases each: Club Soda, Seltzer Water, Tonic Water, Ginger Ale, Cola, Beer

Beware: In today's society, it is not uncommon for the hosts of a party to be held legally responsible for the conduct and safety of their guests. Keep this in mind when planning the quantity and type of beverages to serve. Also, be sure to remind your bartenders not to serve alcohol to minors.

Tips To Save Money: To keep beverage costs down, serve punch, wine, or nonalcoholic drinks only. If your caterer allows it, consider buying liquor from a wholesaler who will let you return unopened bottles. Also, avoid salty foods such as potato chips, pretzels or ham. These foods will make your guests thirstier so they will tend to drink more.

Host alcoholic beverages for the first hour, then go to a cash bar. Or host beer, wine, and soft drinks only and have mixed drinks available on a cash basis. The bartending fee is often waived if you meet the minimum requirements on beverages consumed. For the toast, tray pass champagne only to those guests who want it, not to everyone. Many people will make a toast with whatever they are currently drinking. Consider serving sparkling cider in place of champagne.

Omit waiters and waitresses. Instead, have an open bar in which your guests have to get their own drinks. People tend to drink almost twice as much if there are waiters and waitresses constantly asking them if they would like another drink and then bringing drinks to them.

Price Range: $8 - $25/person

BARTENDING / BAR SET-UP FEE

Some reception sites and caterers charge an extra fee for bartending and for setting up the bar.

Tips To Save Money: The bartending fee could be and often is waived if you meet a minimum requirement on beverages consumed. Try to negotiate this with your caterer prior to hiring him/her.

Price Range: $50 - $375

CORKAGE FEE

Many reception sites and caterers make money by marking up the food and alcohol they sell. You may wish to provide your own alcohol for several reasons. First, it is more cost effective. Second, you may want to serve an exotic wine or champagne that the reception site or caterer does not offer. In either case, and if your reception site or caterer allows it, be prepared to pay a corkage fee. This is the fee for each bottle brought into the reception and opened by a member of their staff.

Things To Consider: You need to consider whether the expenses saved after paying the corkage fee justify the hassle and liability of bringing in your own alcohol.

Price Range: $5 - $10/bottle

FEE TO POUR COFFEE

In addition to the corkage and cake-cutting fees, some facilities also charge extra to pour coffee with the wedding cake.

Things To Consider: Again, when comparing the cost of various reception sites, don't forget to add up all the extra miscellaneous costs, such as the fee for pouring coffee.

Price Range: $0.25 - $0.75/person

SERVICE PROVIDERS' MEALS

Service providers' meals are meals you serve your hired wedding professionals at the reception.

Things To Consider: It is considered a courtesy to feed your photographer, videographer, and any other "service provider" at the reception. Check options and prices with your caterer or reception site manager. Make sure you allocate a place for your service providers to eat. You may want them to eat with your guests, or you may prefer setting a place outside the main room for them to eat. Your service providers may be more comfortable with the latter.

Tips To Save Money: You don't need to feed your service providers the same meal as your guests. You can order sandwiches or another less expensive meal for them. If the meal is a buffet, there should be enough food left after all your guests have been served for your service providers to eat. Tell them they are welcome to eat after all your guests have been served. If this is the case, you may not be charged extra for your service providers to eat. Be sure to discuss this with your catering manager.

Price Range: $7 - $25/person

GRATUITY

It is customary to pay a gratuity fee to your caterer. The average gratuity is 15% to 18% of your food and beverage bill.

Tips To Save Money: Gratuities can range from 15% to 25%. Ask about these costs up front and select your caterer or reception site accordingly.

Price Range: 15% - 18%

PARTY FAVORS

Party favors are little gift items given to your guests as mementos of your wedding. They add a very special touch to your wedding and can become keepsakes for your guests.

Options: White matchboxes engraved with the couple's names; cocktail napkins marked in the same way; individually wrapped and marked chocolates, almonds, or fine candy are all popular party favors. Wine or champagne bottles marked with the bride and groom's names and wedding date on a personalized label are also very popular. These come in different sizes and can be purchased by the case.

If you can afford it, you may also consider porcelain or ceramic party favors. These can be custom-fired with your name and wedding date on them. A new idea that's gaining in popularity among environmentally conscientious couples is to present each guest with a tiny shoot of an endangered tree to be planted in honor of the bride and groom.

Things To Consider: Personalized favors need to be ordered several weeks in advance.

Price Range: $1 - $8/person

DISPOSABLE CAMERAS

A great way to inexpensively obtain many candid photographs of your wedding day is to place a disposable 35 mm camera loaded with film on each table at your reception, and to have your guests take shots of the event! Disposable cameras come pre-loaded with film. Your guests can leave the cameras at their table or drop them in a basket or other labeled container near the entrance to the reception site. Arrange for someone to collect the cameras after the event. Tell your DJ, musician, or wedding coordinator to encourage your guests to take photographs with the disposables. You will end up with many beautiful, memorable and candid photographs of your reception.

Things To Consider: Disposable cameras are sold with and without flash. Disposable cameras with flash are more expensive but necessary if your reception is going to be held indoors or in the evening. If you are planning a large reception, consider buying cameras with only 12 exposures. Otherwise, you may end up with too many photographs. For example, if 200 guests attend your reception and you seat 8 guests per table, you will need to purchase 25 cameras. If each camera has 36 exposures, you will end up with 825 photographs. If the cameras have only 12 exposures, you will end up with 300 photographs, which is a more reasonable quantity!

Tips To Save Money: Instead of developing these photographs into print and then placing them into a big album, have your videographer transfer the negatives directly onto video set to your favorite music. You can then reproduce this "photo montage" and send it as a gift to your friends and family members. You can later decide which of these photographs you want to develop into print.

Price Range: $4 - $13/camera

ROSE PETALS / RICE

Rose petals or rice are traditionally tossed over the bride and groom as they leave the church after the ceremony or when they leave the reception. These are usually handed out to guests in little sachet bags while the bride and groom are changing into their going away clothes. This tradition was initiated in the Middle Ages whereby a handful of wheat was thrown over the bridal couple as a symbol of fertility. Rose petals are used to symbolize happiness, beauty, and prosperity.

Options: Rose petals, rice, or confetti is often used. However, an environmentally correct alternative is to use grass or flower seeds, which do not need to be "cleaned up" if tossed over a grassy area. These come wrapped in attractive, recycled packages with the couple's names and wedding date printed on the front.

Things To Consider: Rose petals can stain carpets; rice can sting faces, harm birds and make stairs dangerously slippery; confetti is messy and hard to clean. Clubs and hotels seldom permit the use of any of these. Ask about their policy.

Price Range: $.35 - $1/person

GIFT ATTENDANT

The gift attendant is responsible for watching over your gifts during the reception so that no one walks away with them. This is necessary only if your reception is held in a public area such as a hotel or outside garden where other people may be walking by. It is not proper to have a friend or family member take on this duty as s/he would not enjoy the reception. The gift attendant should also be responsible for transporting your gifts from the reception to your car or bridal suite.

Tips To Save Money: Hire a young boy or girl from your neighborhood to watch over your gifts at the reception.

Price Range: $20 - $80

PARKING FEE / VALET SERVICES

Many reception sites such as hotels, restaurants, etc. charge for parking. It is customary, although not necessary, for the host of the wedding to pay this charge. At a large home reception, you should consider hiring a professional, qualified valet service if parking could be a problem.   If so, make sure the valet service is fully insured.

Things To Consider: When comparing the cost of reception sites, don't forget to add the cost of parking to the total price.

Tips To Save Money: To save money, let your guests pay their own parking fees.

Price Range: $1.50 - $9/car

*M*USIC

CEREMONY MUSIC

Ceremony music is the music played during the ceremony; i.e., prelude, processional, ceremony, recessional, and postlude. Prelude music is played 15 to 30 minutes before the ceremony begins and while guests are being seated. Processional music is played as the wedding party enters the ceremony site. Ceremony music is played during the ceremony. Recessional music is played as the wedding party leaves the ceremony site. Postlude music is played while guests leave the ceremony site.

Options: The most traditional musical instrument for wedding ceremonies is the organ. But guitars, pianos, flutes, harps and violins are also popular today. The two most popular musical selections for the processional are *Trumpet Voluntary* by Purcell and *The Bridal Chorus* by Wagner. Popular selections for the recessional are *Wedding March* by Mendelssohn and *Postlude in G Major* by Handel. *Canon in D Major* by Pachelbel and *Adagio in A Minor* by Bach are also popular selections for wedding ceremonies.

Popular musical selections for Jewish weddings are Erev Shel Shoshanim, Erev Ba, and Hana' Ava Babanot.

Things To Consider: Music may or may not be included as part of the ceremony site fee. Be sure to check with your ceremony site about restrictions pertaining to music and the availability of musical instruments for your use. Discuss the selection of ceremony music with your officiant and musicians. Make sure the musicians know how to play the selections you request.

When selecting ceremony music, keep in mind the formality of your wedding, your religious affiliation, and the length of the ceremony. Also consider the location and time of day. If the ceremony is outside where there may be other noises such as traffic, wind, or people's voices, or if a large number of guests will be attending your ceremony, consider having the music, your officiant, and your vows amplified. Make sure there are electrical outlets close to where the instruments will be set up.

Questions To Ask: Make sure you ask the following questions to ensure a smart hiring decision:

- What is the name and phone number of my contact person?
- How many years of professional experience do you have?
- What percentage of your business is dedicated to weddings?
- Are you the person who will perform at my wedding?
- What instrument(s) do you play?
- What type of music do you specialize in?
- What are your hourly fees?
- What is your cost for a soloist?
- What is your cost for a duet?

- What is your cost for a trio?
- What is your cost for a quartet?
- How would you dress for my wedding?
- Do you have liability insurance?
- Do you have a cordless microphone?
- What is your payment policy?
- What is your cancellation policy?

Tips To Save Money: Hire student musicians from your local university or high school. Ask a friend to sing or play at your ceremony; they will be honored. If you're planning to hire a band for your reception, consider hiring a scaled-down version of the same band to play at your ceremony, such as a trio of flute, guitar, and vocals. This could enable you to negotiate a "package" price. If you're planning to hire a DJ for your reception, consider hiring him/her to play pre-recorded music at your ceremony.

Price Range: $50 - $400

RECEPTION MUSIC

Music is a major part of your reception, and should be planned carefully. Music helps create the atmosphere of your wedding. Special songs will make your reception unique. When you select music for your reception, keep in mind the age and musical preference of your guests, your budget, and any restrictions that the reception site may have. Bands and musicians are typically more expensive than DJ's.

Options: There are many options for reception music: you can hire a DJ, a band, an orchestra, or any combination of one or more instruments and vocalists.

Things To Consider: Consider hiring an entertainment agency that can help you choose a reliable DJ or band that will play the type of music you want.   Whoever you choose should have experience performing at wedding receptions.

If you want your musician to act as a master of ceremonies, make sure s/he has a complete timeline for your reception so s/he knows when to announce the various events such as the toasts, first dance, and cutting of the cake.   Consider watching your musicians perform at another event before booking their services.

If you need a large variety of music to satisfy all your guests, consider hiring a DJ.   A professional DJ can play any type of music and may even offer a light show.   Make sure you give him/her a list of the songs you want played at your reception and a timeline for playing each one. Make sure there are electrical outlets at the reception site close to where the musicians will be performing.

Questions To Ask: Ask all the following questions to ensure a smart hiring decision:

* What is the name and phone number of my contact person?
* How many years of professional experience do you have?
* How many people are in your band?

- What percentage of your business is dedicated to wedding receptions?
- What type of music do you specialize in?
- What type of sound system do you have?
- Will you perform at my reception?
- Can you act as a master of ceremonies?
- How do you dress for receptions?
- Do you have a cordless microphone?
- Can you provide a light show?
- How many breaks do you take in a 4-hour reception?
- Do you play recorded music during breaks?
- How long are your breaks?
- Do you have liability insurance?
- What are your fees for a 4-hour reception?
- What is your cost per additional hour?
- What is your payment policy?
- What is your cancellation policy?

Tips To Save Money: You will probably get a better price if you hire a band or DJ directly, rather than using an entertainment agency to hire your musicians.

Check the music department of local colleges and universities for names of student musicians and DJ's. You may be able to hire a student for a fraction of the price of a professional musician or DJ.   A DJ is typically less expensive than a "live" musician, saving $200 - $1,000. Some facilities have contracts with certain DJ's, and you may be able to save money by hiring one of them.

Price Range: $300 -$3,000

*P*ERSONAL *N*OTES

$\mathscr{B}$AKERY

WEDDING CAKE

Wedding cakes may be ordered from a caterer or from a bakery. Some hotels and restaurants may also be able to provide a wedding cake. However, you will probably be better off ordering your cake from a bakery that specializes in wedding cakes. Ask to see photographs of other wedding cakes your baker has created, and by all means, ask for a tasting!

Options: When ordering your cake, you will have to decide not only on a flavor, but also on a size, shape and color. Size is determined by the number of guests. You can choose from one large tier to two, three, or more smaller tiers. The cake can be round, square or heart-shaped. The most common flavors are chocolate, carrot, lemon, rum, and "white" cakes. You can be creative by adding a filling to your cake, such as custard, strawberry, or chocolate. You may also want to consider having tiers of different flavors.

Things To Consider: Price, workmanship, quality, and taste vary considerably from baker to baker. In addition to flavor, size, and cost, consider decoration and spoilage (sugar keeps longer than cream frostings). The cake should be beautifully displayed on its own table decorated with flowers or greenery. Make sure the baker, caterer, or reception site manager can provide you with a pretty cake-cutting knife. If not, you will need to purchase or rent one.

When determining the size of the cake to order, don't forget that you'll be saving the top tier for your first anniversary. This top tier should be removed before the cake is cut and then wrapped in several layers of plastic wrap or placed in a sealed plastic container. It should be kept frozen until your anniversary.

Questions To Ask: Be sure to ask all the following questions before selecting a bakery:

- What is the name and phone number of my contact person?
- How many years have you been making wedding cakes?
- What are your wedding cake specialties?
- Do you offer free tasting of your wedding cakes?
- Do you freeze your wedding cakes?
- How far in advance should I order my cake?
- Can you make a groom's cake?
- Do you lend, rent or sell cake knives?
- What is the cost per serving of my desired cake?
- What is your cake pillar and plate rental fee, if any?
- Is this fee refundable upon the return of these items?
- When must these items be returned?
- What is your cake delivery and set-up fee?
- What is your payment policy?
- What is your cancellation policy?

Tips To Save Money: Compare taste, type and quality. Some bakers do not have set-up or delivery fees, some do. Check for individuals who bake from their home. They are usually more reasonable but you should check with the health department where you live. Some caterers have contracts with bakeries and can pass on savings to you.

Some bakeries require a deposit on columns and plates. You lose the deposit if you fail to return these items to the baker within the specified time. Other bakeries use disposable columns and plates, saving you the rental fee and the hassle of returning these items.

Price Range: $1 - $8/piece

GROOM'S CAKE

The groom's cake is an old southern tradition whereby this cake is cut up and distributed to guests in little white boxes engraved with the bride and groom's names. Today the groom's cake, if offered, is cut and served along with the wedding cake.

Options: Usually a chocolate cake decorated with fruit.

Tips To Save Money: Because of its cost and the labor involved in cutting and distributing the cake, very few people offer this delightful custom any more.

Price Range: $0.75 - $1.50/piece

CAKE DELIVERY & SET-UP FEE

This is the fee charged by bakers to deliver and set up your wedding cake at the reception site. It usually includes a deposit on the cake pillars and plate which will be refunded upon their return to the baker.

Tips To Save Money: Have a friend or family member get a quick lesson on how to set up your cake. Have them pick it up and set it up the day of your wedding, then have the florist decorate the cake and/or cake table with flowers and greenery.

Price Range: $20 - $50

CAKE-CUTTING FEE

Most reception sites and caterers charge a fee for each slice of cake they cut if the cake is brought in from an outside bakery. This fee will probably shock you. It is simply their way of enticing you to order the cake through them. And unfortunately, many sites and caterers will not allow a member of your party to cut the cake.

Tips To Save Money: Many hotels and restaurants include a dessert in the cost of their meal packages. If you forego this dessert and substitute your cake as the dessert, they may be willing to waive the cake-cutting fee. Be sure to ask them.

Price Range: $.75 - 1.75/person

CAKE TOP

The bride's cake is often topped and surrounded with fresh flowers, but traditional cake tops are also very popular.

Options: Bells, love birds, a bridal couple or replica of two wedding rings are popular choices for cake tops and can be saved as mementos of your wedding day.

Beware: Some porcelain and other heavier cake tops need to be anchored down into the cake. If you're planning to use a cake top other than flowers, be sure to discuss this with your baker.

Tips To Save Money: Borrow a cake top from a friend or a family member as "something borrowed," an age-old wedding tradition. See "Wedding Traditions" on page 0184.

Price Range: $25 - $150

CAKE KNIFE / TOASTING GLASSES

Your cake knife and toasting glasses should compliment your overall setting; these items will bring you happy memories of your wedding day every time you use them. The cake knife is used to cut the cake at the reception. The bride usually cuts the first two slices of the wedding cake with the groom's hand placed over hers. The groom feeds the bride first, then the bride feeds the groom. This tradition makes beautiful wedding photographs.

You will need toasting glasses to toast each other after you cut the cake. They are usually decorated with ribbons or flowers and kept near the cake. This tradition also makes beautiful wedding photographs.

Things To Consider: Consider having your initials and wedding date engraved on your wedding knife as a memento. Consider purchasing crystal or silver toasting glasses as a keepsake of your wedding. Have your florist decorate your knife and toasting glasses with flowers or ribbons.

Tips To Save Money: Borrow your cake knife or toasting glasses from a friend or family member as "something borrowed," an age-old wedding tradition. See "Wedding Traditions" on page 184. Use the reception facility's glasses and knife, and decorate them with flowers or ribbon.

Price Range: $15 - $120/knife
$30 - $80/toasting glasses

*F*LOWERS

BRIDE'S BOUQUET

The bridal bouquet is one of the most important elements of the bride's attire and deserves special attention. Start by selecting the color and shape of the bouquet. Consider stephanotis -- tradition regards it as the bridal good-luck flower! The bridal bouquet should be carried low enough so that all the intricate details of your gown are visible.

Options: There are many colors, scents, sizes, shapes and styles of bouquets to choose from. The traditional bridal bouquet is made of white flowers. Stephanotis, gardenias, white roses, orchids and lilies of the valley are popular choices for an all-white bouquet.

If you prefer a colorful bouquet, you may want to consider using roses, tulips, stock, peonies, freesias, and Gerbera, which come in a wide variety of colors. Using scented flowers in your bouquet will evoke memories of your wedding day whenever you smell them in the future. Popular fragrant flowers for bouquets are gardenias, freesias, magnolias, and wisteria. Select flowers that are in season to assure availability.

Popular Flowers for a Summer Bouquet:

Allium	Amaryllis	Billy Buttons
Celosia	Dahlia	Delphinium
Liatris	Lisianthus	Pincushion
Queen Anne's Lace	Saponaria	Snapdragon
Speedwell	Sunflower	Tuberose

Popular Flowers for a Fall Bouquet:

Amaryllis	Anemones	Dahlia
Delphinium	Liatris	Lisianthus
Narcissus	Protea	Snapdragon
Star of Bethlehem	Tuberose	

Popular Flowers for a Winter Bouquet:

Amaryllis	Anemone	Narcissus
Protea	Star of Bethlehem	Tulip
Waxflower		

Popular Flowers for a Spring Bouquet:

Allium	Anemone	Billy Buttons
Celosia	Daffodils	Liatris
Lily of the Valley	Lisianthus	Narcissus
Peony	Ranunculus	Snapdragon
Sunflower	Sweet Pea	Tulip
Waxflower		

Popular Flowers Year-Round:

Alstroemeria	Aster	Baby's Breath
Bachelor's Button	Bird of Paradise	Bouvardia
Calla Lily	Carnation	Chrysanthemum
Eucalyptus	Freesia	Gardenia
Gerbera Gladiolus	Iris	Lily Nerine
Orchid	Rose	Statice
Stephanotis	Stock	

Things To Consider: Your flowers should complement the season, your gown, your color scheme, your attendants' attire, and the style and formality of your wedding. If you have a favorite flower, build your bouquet around it and include it in all your arrangements.   Some flowers carry centuries of symbolism.   Pimpernel signifies change; white flowers radiate innocence; forget-me-nots indicate true love; and ivy stands for friendship, fidelity, and matrimony -- the three essentials for a happy marriage.

No flower, however, has as much symbolism for brides as the orange blossom, having at least 700 years of nuptial history. Its unusual ability to simultaneously bear flowers and produce fruit symbolizes the fusion of beauty, personality, and fertility.

Whatever flowers you select, final arrangements should be made well in advance of your wedding date to insure availability. Confirm your final order and delivery time a few days before the wedding. Have the flowers delivered before the photographer arrives so that you can include them in your pre-ceremony photos.

In determining the size of your bouquet, consider your gown and your overall stature. Carry a smaller bouquet if you're petite or if your gown is fairly ornate. A long, cascading bouquet complements a fairly simple gown or a tall or larger bride. Arm bouquets look best when resting naturally in the crook of your arm.

For a natural, fresh-picked look, have your florist put together a cluster of flowers tied together with a ribbon. For a Victorian appeal, carry a nosegay or a basket filled with flowers. Or carry a Bible or other family heirloom decorated with just a few flowers. For a contemporary look, you may want to consider carrying an arrangement of calla lilies or other long-stemmed flower over your arm. For a dramatic statement, carry a single stem of your favorite flower!

Questions To Ask: Be sure you ask all the following questions before selecting a florist:

- What is the name and phone number of my contact person?
- How many years of professional floral experience do you have?
- What percentage of your business is dedicated to weddings?
- Do you have access to out-of-season flowers?
- Will you visit the ceremony and reception sites to make floral recommendations?
- Can you preserve my bridal bouquet?
- Do you rent vases and candleholders?
- Can you provide silk flowers?

- What is your cost of a bridal bouquet made of a dozen white roses and stephanotis?
- What is your cost of a boutonniere made of a single white rose?
- What is your cost of a corsage made with two gardenias?
- Do you have liability insurance?
- What is your delivery and set-up fee?
- What is your payment policy?
- What is your cancellation policy?
- Do you accept credit cards?
- What are your hours?

Beware: If your bouquet includes delicate flowers that will not withstand hours of heat or a lack of water, make sure your florist uses a bouquet holder to keep them fresh. If you want to carry fresh-cut stems without a bouquet holder, make sure the flowers you select are hardy enough to go without water for the duration of your ceremony and reception.

Tips To Save Money: The cost of some flowers may be significantly higher during their off-season. So try to select flowers which are in bloom and plentiful at the time of your wedding. Avoid exotic, out-of-season flowers. Allow your florist to emphasize your colors using more reasonable, seasonal flowers to achieve your total look. If you have a favorite flower that is costly or out of season, consider using silk for that one flower.

Avoid scheduling your wedding on holidays such as Valentine's Day and Mother's Day when the price of flowers is higher. Because every attendant will carry or wear flowers, consider keeping the size of your wedding party down to accommodate your floral budget. Hire a florist who works from his/her home.

Price Range: - $60 - $500

TOSSING BOUQUET

If you want to preserve your bridal bouquet, consider having your florist make a smaller, less expensive bouquet specifically for tossing. This will be the bouquet you toss to your single, female friends toward the end of the reception. Tradition has it that the woman who catches the bouquet is the next to be married. Have your florist include a few sprigs of fresh ivy in the tossing bouquet to symbolize friendship and fidelity.

Tips To Save Money: Use the floral cake top or guest book table "tickler bouquet" as the tossing bouquet. Or omit the tossing bouquet altogether and simply toss your bridal bouquet.

Price Range: $10 - $30

MAID OF HONOR'S BOUQUET

The maid of honor's bouquet can be somewhat larger or a different color than the rest of the bridesmaids' bouquets. This will help to set her apart from the others.

Price Range: $25 - $75

BRIDESMAIDS' BOUQUETS

The bridesmaids' bouquets should complement the bridal bouquet but are generally smaller in size. The size and color should coordinate with the bridesmaids' dresses and the overall style of the wedding. Bridesmaids' bouquets are usually identical.

Options: To personalize your bridesmaids' bouquets, insert a different flower in each of their bouquets to make a statement. For example, if one of your bridesmaids has been sad, give her a lily of the valley to symbolize the return of happiness. To tell a friend that you admire her, insert yellow jasmine. A pansy will let your friend know that you are thinking of her.

Things To Consider: Choose a bouquet style (cascade, cluster, contemporary, hand-tied) that compliments the formality of your wedding and the height of your attendants. If your bridesmaids will be wearing floral print dresses, select flowers that complement the floral print.

Tips To Save Money: Have your attendants carry a single stemmed rose, lily or other suitable flower for an elegant look that also saves money.

Price Range: $15 - $60

MAID OF HONOR / BRIDESMAIDS' HAIRPIECE

For a garden-look, have your maid of honor and brides-maids wear garlands of flowers in their hair. If so, provide your maid of honor with a slightly different color or variety of flower to set her apart from the others.

Options: You may consider using artificial flowers for the hairpieces as long as they are in keeping with the flowers carried by members of the bridal party. Since it is not always easy to find good artificial blooms, other types of hairpieces may be more satisfactory, durable, and attractive.

Things To Consider: Flowers used for the hairpiece must be a sturdy and long-lived variety.

Price Range: $8 - $25

FLOWER GIRL'S HAIRPIECE

Flower girls often wear a wreath of flowers as a hairpiece.

Options: This is another place where artificial flowers may be used, but they must be in keeping with the flowers carried by members of the bridal party. Since it is not always easy to find good artificial blooms, other types of hairpieces may be more satisfactory, durable, and attractive.

Things To Consider: If the flowers used for the hair-piece are not of a sturdy and long-lived variety, a ribbon, bow, or hat might be a safer choice.

Price Range: $8 - $25

BRIDE'S GOING AWAY CORSAGE

You may want to consider wearing a corsage on your going-away outfit. This makes for pretty photos as you and your new husband leave the reception for your honeymoon. Have your florist create a corsage which echoes the beauty of your bouquet.

Beware: Put a protective shield under lilies when using them as corsages, as their anthers will easily stain fabric. Be careful when using Alstroemeria as corsages, as its sap can be harmful if it enters the human bloodstream.

Tips To Save Money: Ask your florist if s/he can design your bridal bouquet in such a way that the center flowers may be removed and worn as a corsage. Or omit this corsage altogether.

Price Range: $10 - $25

OTHER FAMILY MEMBERS' CORSAGES

The groom is responsible for providing flowers for his mother, the bride's mother, and the grandmothers. The officiant, if female, may also be given a corsage to reflect her important role in the ceremony. The corsages don't have to be identical, but they should be coordinated with the color of their dresses.

Options: The groom may order flowers that can be pinned to a pocketbook or worn around a wrist.   He should ask which style the women prefer, and if a particular color is needed to coordinate with their dresses. Gardenias, camellias, white orchids, or Cymbidium orchids are excellent choices for corsages, as they go well with any outfit.

Things To Consider: The groom may also want to consider ordering corsages for other close family members, such as sisters and aunts. This will add a little to your floral expenses, but will make these female family members feel more included in your wedding and will let guests know that they are related to the bride and groom. Many women do not like to wear corsages, so the groom should check with them before ordering the flowers.

Beware: Put a protective shield under lilies when using them as corsages, as their anthers will easily stain fabric. Be careful when using Alstroemeria as corsages, as its sap can be harmful if it enters the human bloodstream.

Tips To Save Money: Ask your florist to recommend reasonable flowers for corsages. Dendrobium orchids are reasonable and make lovely corsages.

Price Range: $10 - $25

GROOM'S BOUTONNIERE

The groom wears his boutonniere on the left lapel, nearest to his heart.

Options: Boutonnieres are generally a single blossom such as a rosebud, stephanotis, freesia or a miniature carnation. If a rosebud is used for the wedding party, have the groom wear two rosebuds, or add a sprig of baby's breath to differentiate him from the groomsmen.

Things To Consider: Consider using a small cluster of flowers instead of a single bloom for the groom's boutonniere.

Beware: Be careful when using Alstroemeria as a boutonniere, as its sap can be harmful if it enters the human bloodstream.

Tips To Save Money: Use mini-carnations rather than roses.

Price Range: $4 - $10

USHERS AND OTHER FAMILY MEMBERS' BOUTONNIERES

The groom gives each man in his wedding party a boutonniere to wear on his left lapel. The officiant, if male, may also be given a boutonniere to reflect his important role in the ceremony. The ring bearer may or may not wear a boutonniere, depending on his outfit.   A boutonniere is more appropriate on a tuxedo than on knickers and knee socks.

Options: Generally, a single blossom such as a rosebud, freesia, or miniature carnation is used as a boutonniere.

Things To Consider: The groom should also consider ordering boutonnieres for other close family members such as fathers, grandfathers, and brothers. This will add a little to your floral expenses, but will make these male family members feel more included in your wedding and will let guests know that they are related to the bride and groom.

Beware: Be careful when using Alstroemeria as boutonnieres, as its sap can be harmful if it enters the human bloodstream.

Tips To Save Money: Use mini-carnations rather than roses.

Price Range: $3 - $7

MAIN ALTAR

The purpose of flowers at the main altar is to direct the guests' visual attention toward the front of the church or synagogue and to the bridal couple. Therefore, they must be seen by guests seated in the back. The flowers for the ceremony site can be as elaborate or as simple as you wish. Your officiant's advice, or that of the altar guild or florist, can be most helpful in choosing flowers for the altar and chancel.

Options: If your ceremony is outside, decorate the arch, gazebo, or other structure serving as the altar with flowers or greenery. In a Jewish ceremony, vows are said under a Chuppah, which is placed at the altar and covered with greens and fresh flowers.

Things To Consider: In choosing floral accents, consider the decor of your ceremony site. Some churches and synagogues are ornate enough and don't need extra flowers. Too many arrangements would get lost in the architectural splendor. Select a few dramatic showpieces that will complement the existing decor. Be sure to ask if there are any restrictions on flowers at the church or synagogue. Remember, decorations should be determined by the size and style of the building, the formality of the wedding, the preferences of the bride, the cost, and the regulations of the particular site.

Tips To Save Money: Decorate the ceremony site with greenery only. Candlelight and greenery are elegant in and of themselves. Use greenery and flowers from your garden. Have your ceremony outside in a beautiful garden or by the water, surrounded by nature's own splendor.

Price Range: $50 - $1,000

ALTAR CANDELABRA

In a candlelight ceremony, the candelabra may be decorated with flowers or greens for a dramatic effect.

Options: Ivy may be twined around the candelabra, or flowers may be strung to them.

Price Range: $25 - $50

AISLE PEWS

Flowers, candles or ribbons are often used to mark the aisle pews and add color.

Options: A cluster of flowers, a cascade of greens, or a cascade of flowers and ribbons are all popular choices for aisle pew decorations. Candles with adorning greenery add an elegant touch.

Things To Consider: Use hardy flowers that can tolerate being handled as pew ornaments. Gardenias and camellias, for example, are too sensitive to last long.

Beware: Avoid using Allium as aisle pew decorations as it has an odor of onions.

Tips To Save Money: It is not necessary to decorate all of the aisle pews, if any at all. To save money, decorate only the reserved family pews. Or decorate every second or third pew.

Price Range: $5 - $40

RECEPTION SITE

Flowers add beauty, fragrance, and color to your reception. Flowers for the reception, like everything else, should fit your style and color scheme. Flowers can help transform a stark reception hall into a warm, inviting and colorful room.

Options: For an evening reception, use votive candles wherever possible to create a warm, romantic setting -- along walkways, around a pool, in bathrooms, etc. Use twinkle lights to achieve a magical effect. Place them on indoor or outdoor trees.

Things To Consider: Consider renting indoor plants or small trees to give your reception a garden-like atmosphere.

Tips To Save Money: You can save money by taking flowers from the ceremony to decorate the reception site. However, you must coordinate this move carefully to avoid having your guests arrive at an undecorated reception room. Use greenery to fill large areas. Trees and garlands of ivy can give a dramatic impact for little money. Use greenery and flowers from your garden. Have your reception outside in a beautiful garden or by the water, surrounded by nature's own beauty.

Price Range: $300 - $1,500

HEAD TABLE

The head table is where the wedding party will sit during the reception. This important table should be decorated with a larger, more dramatic centerpiece than the guest tables.

Things To Consider: Consider using a different color or style of arrangement to set the head table apart from the other tables.

Beware: Avoid using fragrant flowers, such as Allium or Narcissus, on tables where food is being served or eaten, as their fragrance may conflict with other aromas.

Tips To Save Money: Decorate the head table with the bridal and attendants' bouquets.

Price Range: $50 - $300

GUEST TABLES

At a reception where guests are seated, a small flower arrangement may be placed on each table.

Things To Consider: The arrangements should complement the table linens and the size of the table, and should be kept low enough so as not to hinder conversation among guests seated across from each other.

Beware: Avoid using highly fragrant flowers on tables where food is being served or eaten.

Tips To Save Money: To keep the cost down and for less formal receptions, use small potted flowering plants placed in white baskets, or consider using dried or silk arrangements that you can make yourself and give later as gifts. Or place a wreath of greenery entwined with colored ribbon in the center of the table. Use a different colored ribbon at each table and assign your guests to tables by ribbon color rather than by number.

Price Range: $10 - $60

BUFFET TABLE

If buffet tables are used, have some type of floral arrangement on the tables to add color and beauty to your display of food.

Options: Whole fruits and bunches of berries offer a variety of design possibilities. Figs add a festive touch. Pineapples are a sign of hospitality. Vegetables offer an endless array of options to decorate with. Herbs are yet another option in decorating. A mixture of rosemary and mint combined with scented geraniums makes a very unique table decoration.

Things To Consider: Depending on the size of the table, place one or two arrangements at each side.

Beware: Avoid placing carnations, snapdragons, and Star of Bethlehem next to buffet displays of fruits or vegetables, as these flowers are extremely sensitive to the gasses emitted by these foods.

Price Range: $50 - $300

PUNCH TABLE

Put an assortment of greens or a small arrangement of flowers at the punch table. See "Buffet Table," on page 149.

Price Range: $10 - $50

CAKE TABLE

The wedding cake is often the central location at the reception. Decorate the cake table with flowers.

Tips To Save Money: Have your bridesmaids place their bouquets on the cake table during the reception. Or decorate the cake top only and cover the base with greenery.

Price Range: $15 - $25

CAKE

Flowers are a beautiful addition to a wedding cake and are commonly seen spilling out between the cake tiers.

Things To Consider: Use only nonpoisonous flowers, and have your florist - not the caterer - design the floral decorations for your cake. A florist will be able to blend the cake decorations into your overall floral theme.

Price Range: $20 - $60

CAKE KNIFE

Decorate your cake knife with white ribbon and flowers.

Things To Consider: Consider engraving the cake knife with your names and wedding date.

Price Range: $5 - $20

TOASTING GLASSES

Tie small flowers with white ribbons on the stems of your champagne glasses. These wedding accessories deserve a special floral touch since they will most likely be included in your special photographs.

Things To Consider: Consider engraving your toasting glasses with your names and wedding date.

Price Range: $10 - $30

FLORAL DELIVERY & SET-UP

Most florists charge a fee to deliver flowers to the ceremony and reception sites and to arrange them on site.

Things To Consider: Make sure your florist knows where your sites are and what time to arrive.

Price Range: $25 - $100

DECORATIONS

TABLE CENTERPIECES

Each of the tables at your reception, including the head table, should be decorated with a centerpiece.

Options: Candles, mirrors and flowers are popular choices for table centerpieces. However, the options are endless. Just be creative! An arrangement of shells, for example, makes a very nice centerpiece for a seaside reception. Votive candles set on top of a mirror make a romantic centerpiece for an evening reception.

A wreath of greenery woven with colored ribbon makes a delightful centerpiece. Use a different color ribbon at each table and have your guests seated according to ribbon color!

Things To Consider: Select a table centerpiece which complements your colors and/or setting. The centerpiece for the head table should be larger or more elaborate than for the other tables. Make sure that your centerpiece is kept low enough so as not to hinder conversation among guests seated across from each other. Consider using a centerpiece that your guests can take home as a memento of your wedding.

Tips To Save Money: Make your own table centerpieces using materials that are not expensive.

Price Range: $5 - $30 each

BALLOONS

Balloons are often used to decorate a reception site. A popular idea is to release balloons at the church or reception. This adds a festive, exciting, and memorable touch to your wedding. Balloons can be used to create an arch backdrop for the wedding cake or inexpensive centerpieces for the tables.

Things To Consider: Color coordinate your balloons to match your wedding color scheme. Choose colors from your bouquet or your bridesmaids' dresses. Balloons should be delivered and set up well in advance -- at least before the photographer shows up.

If you are planning to release balloons at the church or reception, check with your city. Releasing balloons in some cities might be illegal. Also make sure there are no wires in which balloons can get entangled. If they do, you could be held responsible for damages or cleanup expenses.

Tips To Save Money: Balloons are less expensive than fresh flowers and can be used as a substitute for flowers to decorate the reception site.

Price Range: $75 - $500

*T*RANSPORTATION

TRANSPORTATION

It is customary for the bride and her father to ride to the ceremony site together on the wedding day. You may also include some or all members of your wedding party. Normally a procession to the church begins with the bride's mother and several of the bride's attendants in the first vehicle. If desired, you can provide a second vehicle for the rest of the attendants. The bride and her father will go in the last vehicle. This vehicle will also be used to transport the bride and groom to the reception site after the ceremony.

Options: There are various options for transportation. The most popular choice is a limousine since it is big and open and can accommodate several people as well as your bridal gown. You can also choose to rent a car that symbolizes your personality as a couple.

There are luxury cars such as Mercedes Benz, sports cars such as a Ferraris, and vintage vehicles such as 1950's Thunderbirds or 1930's Cadillacs. If your ceremony and reception sites are fairly close together, and if weather permits, you might want to consider a more romantic form of transportation, such as a horse-drawn carriage.

Things To Consider: In some parts of the country, limousines are booked on a 3-hour minimum basis.

Questions To Ask: Make sure you ask all the following questions before selecting a transportation company:

- What is the name and phone number of my contact person?
- How many years have you been in business?
- How many vehicles do you have available?
- Can you provide a back-up vehicle in case of an emergency?
- What are the brand names of the vehicles available?
- What are the various sizes of vehicles available?
- How old are the vehicles?
- How many drivers are available?
- Can you show me photos of your drivers?
- How do your drivers dress for weddings?
- Do you have liability insurance?
- What is the minimum amount of time required to rent a vehicle?
- What is the cost per hour? Two hours? Three hours?
- How much gratuity is expected?
- What is your payment policy?
- What is your cancellation policy?

Beware: Make sure the company you choose is fully licensed and has liability insurance. Do not pay the full amount until after the event.

Tips To Save Money: Consider hiring only one large limousine. This limousine can transport you, your parents

and your attendants to the ceremony, and then you and
your new husband from the ceremony to the reception.

Price Range: $35 - $100/hour

Personal Notes

RENTAL ITEMS

BRIDAL SLIP RENTAL

The bridal slip is an undergarment which gives the bridal gown its proper shape.

Things To Consider: Be sure to wear the same slip you'll be wearing on your wedding day during your fittings. Many bridal salons rent slips. Schedule an appointment to pick up your slip one week before the wedding; otherwise, there might not be one available on your wedding day. If rented, the slip will have to be returned shortly after the wedding. Arrange for someone to do this for you within the allotted time.

Tips To Save Money: Rent a slip rather than purchasing one; chances are you will never use it again.

Price Range: $15 - $45

CEREMONY ACCESSORIES

Ceremony rental accessories are additional items needed for the ceremony but not included in the ceremony site fee.

Options: Ceremony rental accessories may include the following items:

Aisle Runner:	A thin rug made of plastic, paper or cloth extending the length of the aisle. It is rolled out after the mothers are seated, just prior to the processional. Plastic or paper doesn't work well on grass; but if you must use one of these types of runners, make sure the grass is clipped short.
Kneeling Cushion:	A small cushion or pillow placed in front of the altar where the bride and groom kneel for their wedding blessing.
Arch (Christian):	A white lattice or brass arch where the bride and groom exchange their vows, often decorated with flowers and greenery.
Chuppah (Jewish):	A canopy under which a Jewish ceremony is performed, symbolizing cohabitation and consummation.

You may also need to consider renting audio equipment, aisle stanchions, candelabra, candles, candlelighters, chairs, heaters, a gift table, a guest book stand, and a canopy.

Things To Consider: If you plan to rent any accessories for your ceremony, make sure the rental supplier has been in business for a reasonable period of time and has a good reputation. Reserve the items you need well in advance. Find out the company's payment, reservation and cancellation policies.

Some companies allow you to reserve emergency items such as heaters or canopies without having to pay for them unless needed, in which case you would need to call the rental company a day or two in advance to request the items. If someone else requests the items you have reserved, the company should give you the right of first refusal.

Questions To Ask: Make sure you ask the following questions before selecting a rental supplier for your ceremony or reception:

- What is the name and phone number of my contact person?
- How many years have you been in business?
- What are your hours of operation?
- Do you have liability insurance?
- What is the cost per item needed?
- What is the cost of pick-up and delivery?
- What is the cost of setting up the items rented?
- When would the items be delivered?
- When would the items be picked up after the event?
- What is your payment policy?
- What is your cancellation policy?

Tips To Save Money: When considering a ceremony outside of a church, figure the cost of rental items. Negotiate a package deal, if possible, by renting items for both the ceremony and the reception from the same supplier. Consider renting these items from your florist so you only have to pay one delivery fee.

Price Range: $100 - $400

TENT / CANOPY

A large tent or canopy may be required for receptions held outdoors to protect you and your guests from the sun or rain. Usually rented through party rental suppliers, tents and canopies can be expensive due to the labor involved in delivery and set-up.

Options: Tents and canopies come in different sizes and colors. Depending on the shape of your reception area, you may need to rent several smaller canopies rather than one large one. Contact several party rental suppliers to discuss the options.

Things To Consider: Consider this cost when making a decision between an outdoor and an indoor reception. In cooler weather, heaters may also be necessary.

Tips To Save Money: Shop early and compare prices with several party rental suppliers.

Price Range: $300 - $3,000

DANCE FLOOR

A dance floor will be provided by most hotels and clubs. However, if your reception site does not have a dance floor, you may need to rent one through your caterer or a party rental supplier.

Things To Consider: When comparing prices of dance floors, include the delivery and set-up fees.

Price Range: $100 - $300

TABLES / CHAIRS

You will have to provide tables and chairs for your guests if your reception site or caterer doesn't provide them as part of their package. For a full meal, you will have to provide tables and seating for all guests. For a cocktail reception, you only need to provide tables and chairs for approximately 30 to 50 percent of your guests. Ask your caterer or reception site manager for advice.

Options: There are various types of tables and chairs to choose from. The most common chairs for wedding receptions are white wooden or plastic chairs. The most common tables for receptions are round tables that seat 8 guests. The most common head table arrangement is several rectangular tables placed end-to-end to seat your entire wedding party on one side, facing your guests. Contact various party rental suppliers to find out what types of chairs and tables they carry as well as their price ranges.

Things To Consider: When comparing prices of renting tables and chairs, include the cost of delivery and set-up.

Tips To Save Money: Attempt to negotiate free delivery and set-up with party rental suppliers in exchange for giving them your business.

Price Range: $3 - $8/person

LINEN / TABLEWARE

You will also need to provide linens and tableware for your reception if your reception site or caterer doesn't provide them as part of their package.

Options: For a sit-down reception where the meal is served by waiters and waitresses, tables are usually set with a cloth (usually white, but may be color coordinated with the wedding), a centerpiece, and complete place settings. At a less formal buffet reception where guests serve themselves, tables are covered with a cloth but place settings are not mandatory. The necessary plates and silverware may be located at the buffet table, next to the food.

Things To Consider: Linens and tableware depend on the formality of your reception. When comparing prices, include the cost of delivery and set-up.

Price Range: $3 -$20/person

HEATERS

You may need to rent heaters if your reception will be held outdoors and if the temperature may drop below sixty-five degrees.

Options: There are electric and gas heaters, both of which come in different sizes. Gas heaters are more popular since they do not have unsightly and unsafe electric cords.

Price Range: $25 - $50

LANTERNS

Lanterns are often used at evening receptions.

Options: Many choices are available, from fire lanterns to electric ones.

Things To Consider: Consider the formality of the reception and choose the proper lighting to complement your decorations.

Price Range: $6 - $40/lamp

OTHER RENTAL ITEMS (TRASH CANS, ETC.)

If your reception site or caterer doesn't provide them, you will need to purchase, rent or borrow other miscellaneous items for your reception, such as trash cans, a gift table, trash bags, and so on.

$\mathscr{G}$IFTS

BRIDE'S GIFT

The bride's gift is traditionally given by the groom to the bride. It is typically a personal gift such as a piece of jewelry.

Options: A string of pearls, a watch, pearl earrings, or a gold chain with a heart-shaped charm holding photos of the two of you.

Things To Consider: This gift is not necessary and should be given only if budget allows.

Tips To Save Money: Consider omitting this gift. A pretty card from the groom proclaiming his eternal love for the bride is a very special yet inexpensive gift.

Price Range: $50 - $500

GROOM'S GIFT

The groom's gift is traditionally given by the bride to the groom.

Options: A nice watch, an elegant pen set, or a dramatic photo of the bride framed in silver or crystal.

Things To Consider: This gift is not necessary and should be given only if budget allows.

Tips To Save Money: Consider omitting this gift. A pretty card from the bride proclaiming her eternal love for the groom is a very special yet inexpensive gift.

Price Range: $50 - $500

BRIDESMAIDS' GIFTS

Bridesmaids' gifts are given by the bride to her bridesmaids and maid of honor as a permanent keepsake of the wedding.

Options: For bridesmaids' gifts, consider items of jewelry that can be worn both during and after the wedding; silver or crystal frames; or small handbags that the bridesmaids can carry to the wedding, filled with wedding day essentials such as lipstick, nail polish, jewelry, and pantyhose.

Things To Consider: Bridesmaids' gifts are usually presented at the bridesmaids' luncheon, if there is one, or at the rehearsal dinner. The gift to the maid of honor may be similar to the bridesmaids' gifts but should be a bit more expensive.

Tips To Save Money: Ask your photographer to take, at no extra charge, professional portraits of each bridesmaid and her escort for use as bridesmaids' gifts. Select a beautiful background that will remind your bridesmaids of the occasion, such as your cake table. Put the photo in a pretty frame. This makes a very special yet inexpensive gift for your attendants.

Price Range: $25 - $100/gift

USHERS' GIFTS

Ushers' gifts are given by the groom to his ushers as a permanent keepsake of the wedding.

Options: For ushers' gifts, consider fancy pen sets, wallets, leather belts, silver frames, watches, and desk clocks.

Things To Consider: The groom should deliver his gifts to the ushers at the bachelor party or at the rehearsal dinner. The gift to the best man may be similar to the ushers' gifts but should be a bit more expensive.

Tips To Save Money: Negotiate with your photographer to take, at no extra charge, professional portraits of each usher and his escort for use as ushers' gifts. Select a beautiful background that will remind your ushers of the occasion, such as your cake table. This makes a special yet inexpensive gift for your attendants.

Price Range: $25 - $100/gift

PERSONAL NOTES

*P*ARTIES

BRIDESMAIDS' LUNCHEON

The bridesmaids' luncheon is given by the bride for her bridesmaids. It is not a shower; rather, it is simply a time for good friends to get together formally before the bride changes her status from single to married.

Things To Consider: You can give your bridesmaids their gifts at this gathering. Otherwise, plan to give them their gifts at the rehearsal dinner.

Price Range: $12 - $30/meal

REHEARSAL DINNER

It is customary that the groom's parents host a dinner party following the rehearsal, the evening before the wedding. The dinner usually includes the bridal party, their spouses or guests, both sets of parents, close family members, the officiant, and the wedding consultant and/or coordinator.

Options: The rehearsal dinner party can be held just about anywhere, from a restaurant, hotel, or private hall to the groom's parents' home. Close relatives and out-of-town guests may be included if budget permits.

Tips To Save Money: Restaurants specializing in Mexican food or pizza are fun yet inexpensive options for a casual rehearsal dinner.

Price Range: $10 - $30/person

*M*ISCELLANEOUS

NEWSPAPER ANNOUNCEMENTS

There are two types of announcements you can send to your local newspaper: one to announce your engagement, and one to announce your wedding.

For your engagement announcement, send information to the newspapers, along with a photograph, right after your engagement or at least 4 to 6 weeks before the wedding. The photograph is usually the head and shoulders of the engaged couple. The photograph should be wallet-sized or larger, black and white, and glossy. Call your local newspapers to ask about their requirements. Most papers will not take orders over the phone, so you will need to mail the information or deliver it personally.

For your wedding announcement, send information to the newspapers, along with a photograph of either the bride alone or the bridal couple, at least three weeks before the wedding. The photograph should be wallet-sized or larger, black and white, and glossy. Your photograph should show the way you will look the day of your wedding. The announcement should appear the day following the ceremony.

Things To Consider: If you and your fiancé grew up in different towns, consider sending announcements to the local papers of both towns. If either of you is having second thoughts about the wedding, cancel both announcements as soon as possible.

Tips To Save Money: If you don't mind having your wedding announced a few weeks after the wedding, you can send a photo from your actual wedding day. This will save you the cost and hassle of dressing up to have your photo taken before the wedding.

Price Range: $40 - $80 (depending on size)

MARRIAGE LICENSE

Marriage license requirements are state-regulated and may be obtained from the County Clerk in most county courthouses.

Options: Some states (California and Nevada, for example) offer two types of marriage licenses: a public license and a confidential one. The public license is the most common one and requires a health certificate and a blood test. It can only be obtained at the County Clerk's office.

The confidential license is usually less expensive and does not require a health certificate or blood test. If offered, it can usually be obtained from most Justices of the Peace. An oath must be taken in order to receive either license.

Things To Consider: Requirements vary from state to state but generally include the following points:

1.   Applying for and paying the fee for the marriage license.   There is usually a waiting period before the license is valid and a limited time before it expires.

2.   Meeting residency requirements for the state and/or county where the ceremony will take place.

3.   Meeting the legal age requirements for both bride and groom or having parental consent.

4.   Presenting any required identification, birth or baptismal certificates, marriage eligibility or other documents.

5.   Obtaining a medical examination and/or blood test for both the bride and groom to detect communicable diseases.

Price Range: $20 - $85

PRENUPTIAL AGREEMENT

A prenuptial agreement is a legal contract between the bride and groom itemizing the property each brings into the marriage and explaining how those properties will be divided in case of divorce or death.   Although you can write your own agreement, it is advisable to have an attorney draw up or review the document.   The two of you should be represented by different attorneys.

Things To Consider: Consider a prenuptial agreement if one or both of you have a significant amount of capital or assets, or if there are children involved from a previous marriage. If you are going to live in a different state after the wedding, consider having an attorney from that state draw up or review your document.

Nobody likes to talk about divorce or death when planning a wedding, but it is very important to give these issues your utmost consideration. By drawing a prenuptial agreement, you encourage open communication and get a better idea of each other's needs and expectations. You should also consider drawing up or reviewing your wills at this time.

Tips To Save Money: Some software packages allow you to write your own will and prenuptial agreement, which can save you substantial attorney's fees. However, if you decide to draw either agreement on your own, you should still have an attorney review it.

Price Range: $500 - $3,000

BRIDAL GOWN PRESERVATION

The pride and joy you will experience in seeing your daughter and/or granddaughter wear your wedding gown on her wedding day will more than justify the expense of having your gown preserved. Bring your gown to a reputable dry cleaning company which specializes in preserving wedding gowns. They will dry clean your dress, vacuum seal it, and place it in an attractive box. By doing this, your gown will be protected from yellowing, falling apart, or getting damaged over the years. Most boxes have a plastic see-through window where you can show the top part of your dress to friends and family members without having to open the vacuum-sealed container.

Tips To Save Money: Some bridal boutiques offer gown preservation. Try to negotiate having your gown preserved for free with the purchase of a wedding gown. It's well worth the try! But remember, get any agreement in writing and be sure to have it signed by either the owner or the manager of the boutique.

Price Range: $100 - $200

BRIDAL BOUQUET PRESERVATION

The bridal bouquet can be preserved to make a beautiful memento of the wedding.

Things To Consider: Have your bouquet dried, mounted, and framed to hang on your wall or to display on an easel in a quiet corner of your home. You can also have an artist paint your bouquet.

Price Range: $100 - $500

WEDDING CONSULTANT

Wedding consultants are professionals whose training, expertise, and contacts will help make your wedding as close to perfect as it can possibly be. They can save you considerable time, money and stress when planning your wedding. Wedding consultants have information on many ceremony and reception sites as well as reliable service providers such as photographers, videographers and florists, which will save you hours of investigation and legwork.

Wedding consultants can provide facilities and service providers to match your budget. They can also save you stress by ensuring that what you are planning is correct and that the service providers you hire are reliable and professional. Most service providers recommended by wedding consultants will go out of their way to do an excellent job for you so that the wedding consultant will continue to recommend their services.

Options: You can have a wedding consultant help you do as much or as little as you think necessary. A consultant can help you plan the whole event from the beginning to the end, helping you formulate a budget and select your ceremony and reception sites, flowers, wedding gown, invitations, and service providers; or s/he can help you at the end by coordinating the rehearsal and the wedding day. Remember, you want to feel like a guest at your own wedding. You and your family should not have to worry about any details on that special day.

Things To Consider: Strongly consider engaging the services of a wedding consultant. Contrary to what many people believe, a wedding consultant is part of your wedding budget, not an extra expense! A good wedding consultant should be able to save you at least the amount of his/her fee by suggesting less expensive alternatives that still enhance your wedding. In addition, many consultants obtain discounts from the service providers they work with. If this is not enough, they are more than worth their fee by serving as an intermediary between you and your parents and/or service providers.

When hiring a wedding consultant, make sure you check his/her references. Ask the consultant if s/he is a member of the Association of Bridal Consultants (ABC) and ask to see a current membership certificate. All ABC members agree to uphold a Code of Ethics and Standards of Membership. Many consultants have formal training and experience in event planning and in other specialties related to weddings, such as flower arranging and catering.

Questions To Ask: Be sure you ask all the following questions to ensure a smart hiring decision:

- How many years of professional experience do you have?
- How many consultants are in your company?
- Are you a member of the Association of Bridal Consultants?
- What services do you provide?
- What are your hourly fees?
- What is your fee for complete wedding planning?
- What is your fee for the rehearsal and wedding day?

- What is your payment policy?
- What is your cancellation policy?
- Do you have liability insurance?

Price Range: $400 - $3,000

WEDDING PLANNING SOFTWARE

With a computer, you can ease the process of planning your wedding. A good wedding planning software will help you create a budget, generate a guest list, address invitations, create a wedding timeline or schedule of events, keep track of payments made to service providers, and keep track of invitations sent as well as RSVPs and gifts received.

Options: One of the best wedding planning software programs available is published by Wedding Solutions Publishing, Inc. and is called *Easy Wedding Planning Software for Windows*. This software is very easy to use and will greatly help you plan all aspects of your wedding. You can order this software directly from Wedding Solutions Publishing, Inc. by calling (619) 582-1878 or purchase on-line at *www.yourbridalsuperstore.com*.

Price Range: $30 - $60

TAXES

Don't forget to figure-in the cost of taxes on all taxable items you purchase for your wedding. Many people make a big mistake by not figuring out the taxes they will have to pay for their wedding expenses. For example, if you are planning a reception for 250 guests with an estimated cost of $60/person for food and beverages, your pretax expenses would be $15,000. A sales tax of 7.5% would mean an additional expense of $1,125! Find out what the sales tax is in your area and which items are taxable, and figure this expense into your overall budget.

Personal Notes

Wedding Traditions

Have you ever wondered why certain things are almost always done at weddings? For example, why the bride carries a bouquet or wears a veil? Or why guests throw rice or rose petals over the newlyweds? Everything has a reason. In this section we discuss the origin and symbolism of some of the most popular wedding traditions.

This comprehensive list of wedding traditions comes from a delightful little book entitled *The Romance of the Wedding Ceremony* by Rev. Richleigh Hale Powers, Ph.D. This book has helped many couples personalize their wedding ceremony in a format that is both fun and easy to use.

THE BRIDE'S BOUQUET

Bridal bouquets have evolved through the ages. Saracen brides carried bouquets of orange blossoms to symbolize fertility, and Roman brides carried sheaves of wheat to symbolize prosperity for their husbands. In the eighteenth century, the practice of carrying a bouquet of flowers or herbs became a popular tradition which symbolized fragility, purity, and new life. Bouquets of dill were among the most popular herb carried. After the ceremony the dill was eaten to "provoke lust." Today bridal bouquets are tossed to assembled single women to symbolize new life and to pass on the bride's good fortune.

THE SPECIAL MEANING OF THE BRIDE'S VEIL

The veil represents modesty and respect. It symbolizes the sanctity and exclusiveness of the marriage covenant and reminds the couple and the witnesses that the physical relationship is to be entered into only after the vows are completed.

RICE AND PETALS

In the Middle Ages, handfuls of wheat were thrown over married couples to symbolize the hope for fertility. In modern times, rice is typically thrown as it also symbolizes fertility. In recent years, flower petals have become another alternative, symbolizing beauty, happiness and prosperity.

"SOMETHING OLD, SOMETHING NEW, SOMETHING BORROWED, SOMETHING BLUE"

Old and new items jointly symbolize the passage from the old unmarried state to that of the new married union. The wearing of a borrowed belonging demonstrates community participation in and approval of the wedding. Blue is worn because it is the color that signifies purity, love, and fidelity.

WHITE AISLE RUNNER

A white aisle runner symbolizes walking on holy ground. A marriage covenant is not made merely between two people and their witnesses. It is made in the presence of God and He is actively involved in the agreement. The white aisle runner symbolizes God's holiness.

SPECIAL SEATING FOR THE PARENTS

The parents of the bride and groom are part of the marriage covenant. The commitments they make during the ceremony are just as binding as the vows of the couple. The final responsibility of parents for their children is to determine with them God's will for a life partner. Thereafter, they serve in a chain of counsel for them and their children. Parents enter in the line of authority and leave in the line of counsel.

THE GROOM ENTERING FIRST

By this action the groom signifies that he is the covenant initiator. This is important because whoever initiates the covenant assumes greater responsibility for seeing it fulfilled.

THE FATHER OF THE BRIDE WALKING DOWN THE AISLE

This action has two meanings. By doing so, the father is saying to the bride, "I am endorsing this young man as God's very best choice of a husband for you, and I am now bringing you to him." In addition, the father is saying to the young man, "I am presenting to you a daughter who I have earnestly endeavored to raise as a pure bride."

THE BRIDE AND GROOM TAKING EACH OTHER'S RIGHT HAND DURING THE CEREMONY

The open right hand offered by each party symbolizes their strength, resources and purpose. By clasping each other's right hand, they pledge these qualities to each other so that each partner can depend on all the resources that the other brings into the covenant relationship. The handclasp goes far beyond sealing the contract. It symbolizes the cleaving together of lives which is to be accomplished in the marriage covenant.

THE GROOM MAKING THE FIRST VOW

The groom must be the leader and assume greater responsibility to fulfill the marriage covenant. As covenant initiator, he must commit himself to the purposes of marriage which God established in the beginning. And these must be reflected in his vows.

THE SYMBOLISM OF THE WEDDING RINGS

The wedding rings symbolize the promises binding two people together in marriage. The unbroken circle of the wedding band represents the continuity of undying love. Greek theory believed the fourth finger of the left hand to be connected to the heart, making this the appropriate finger to be "bound" in romantic attachment.

KISSING THE BRIDE

During the Roman empire, the kiss symbolized a legal bond. Continued use of the kiss to seal the marriage bond is based on the deeply rooted idea of the kiss as a vehicle for transference of power and souls.

THE COUPLE BEING PRONOUNCED "HUSBAND AND WIFE"

This establishes their change of names and a definite point in time for the beginning of the marriage. These words are to remove any doubt in the minds of the couple or the witnesses concerning the validity of the marriage.

SIGNING THE WEDDING PAPERS

The newlyweds sign the wedding papers to establish a public document and public record of the covenant.

SIGNING THE GUEST BOOK

Your wedding guests are official witnesses to the covenant. By signing the guest book, they are saying, "I have witnessed the vows, and I will testify to the reality of this marriage." Because of this significance, the guest book should be signed after the wedding rather than before it.

THE PURPOSE OF THE RECEIVING LINE

The receiving line is for guests to give their blessings to the couple and their parents.

THE MEANING OF SERVING FOOD AT THE RECEPTION

Food is part of the covenant celebration. It further symbolizes the unity of the couple. Entering into a meal itself is a form of covenant.

THE BRIDE AND GROOM FEEDING WEDDING CAKE TO EACH OTHER

This represents the sharing of their body to become one. A New Testament illustration of this symbolism is The Lord's Supper.

*D*O'S & *D*ON'TS

Your wedding will last only a few hours but will likely take several months to plan. That is why it is so important to enjoy the complete wedding planning process. This is a time to get excited, to fall even more deeply in love with each other, to learn more about each other and how to give and take. If you can handle your wedding planning with your fiancé and parents, you can handle anything! Here is a list of do's and don'ts when planning your special day. If you follow these suggestions, your wedding planning and your wedding day will be more enjoyable!

DO'S

Read this book completely.

Hire a professional wedding consultant.

Maintain a sense of humor.

Maintain open communication with your fiancé and with both sets of parents, especially if they are financing the wedding.

Be receptive to your parents' ideas, especially if they are financing the wedding.

Be flexible and keep your overall budget in mind.

Maintain a regular routine of exercise and eat a well-balanced diet.

Buy the *Indispensable Groom's Guide,* published by Wedding Solutions Publishing, Inc., and give it to your fiancé.

Buy the *Wedding Party Responsibility Cards,* published by Wedding Solutions Publishing, Inc., and give a card to each member of your wedding party.

Register for gifts; consider a price range that your guests can afford.

Break-in your shoes well before your wedding day.

Practice with makeup and various hairstyles for your wedding day.

Check recent references for all of your service providers.

Get everything in writing with your service providers.

Assign your guests to tables and group them together by age, interests, acquaintances, etc.

Consider drawing-up a prenuptial agreement and a will.

Send thank-you notes as soon as you receive gifts.

Give a rose to each of your mothers as you walk down the aisle during the recessional.

Try to spend some time with each of your guests and personally thank them for coming to your wedding.

Encourage the bride's parents to introduce their family and friends to the family and friends of the groom's family, and vice-versa.

Toast both sets of parents at the rehearsal dinner and/or at the reception. Thank them for everything they have done for you and for giving you a beautiful wedding.

Eat well at the reception, especially if you will be drinking alcohol.

Keep a smile on your face; there will be many photographs taken of both of you.

Expect things to go wrong on your wedding day. Most likely something will go wrong, and no one will notice it but yourself. Relax and don't let it bother you.

Preserve the top tier of your wedding cake for your first year anniversary.

Send a special gift to both sets of parents, such as a small album containing the best photographs of the wedding. Personalize this gift by having it engraved with your names and the date of your wedding.

DON'TS

Don't get involved in other activities; you will be very busy planning your wedding.

Don't make any major decisions without discussing it openly with your fiancé.

Don't be controlling. Be open to other people's ideas.

Don't overspend your budget; this can be extremely stressful.

Don't wait until the last minute to hire your service providers. The good ones get booked months in advance.

Don't try to make everyone happy; it is impossible and will only make your wedding planning more difficult.

Don't try to impress your friends.

Don't invite old boyfriends or girlfriends to your wedding; you don't want to make anybody uncomfortable.

Don't try to do "everything." Delegate responsibilities to your fiancé, your parents, and to members of your wedding party.

Don't rely on friends or family to photograph or videotape your wedding. Hire professionals!

Don't assume that members of your wedding party know what to do. Give them direction with the *Wedding Party*

Responsibility Cards, available at most major bookstores and at *www.yourbridalsuperstore.com*.

Don't assume your service providers know what to do.

Don't schedule your bachelor party the night before the wedding. You don't want to have a hangover on your special day!

Don't arrive late at the ceremony!

Don't get drunk during your reception; you don't want to make a fool of yourself on your most special day.

Don't flirt with members of the opposite sex.

Don't allow your guests to drive drunk after the reception; you may be held responsible.

Don't rub cake in the face of your spouse during the cake-cutting ceremony; your spouse might not appreciate it!

Don't overeat; this may upset your stomach or make you sleepy.

Don't leave your reception without saying good-bye to your family and friends.

Don't drive if you have had too much to drink.

Personal Notes

WEDDING PARTY RESPONSIBILITIES

Each member of your wedding party has his/her own individual duties and responsibilities. The following is a list of the most important duties for each member of your wedding party.

The most convenient method for conveying this information to members of your wedding party is by purchasing a set of the *Wedding Party Responsibility Cards*, published by Wedding Solutions Publishing, Inc.. These cards are available at most major bookstores. They can also be ordered on-line at *www.yourbridalsuperstore.com*.

These cards are very attractive and contain all the information your wedding party needs to know to assure a smooth wedding; i.e., what to do, how to do it, when to do it, when to arrive, and much more. They also include financial responsibilities as well as the processional, recessional and altar line-ups.

Maid of Honor

- Helps bride select attire and address invitations.
- Plans bridal shower for bride.
- Arrives at dressing site 2 hours before ceremony to assist bride in dressing.
- Arrives dressed at ceremony site 1 hour before the wedding for photographs.
- Arranges the bride's veil and train before the processional and recessional.
- Holds bride's bouquet and groom's ring, if no ring bearer, during the ceremony.
- Witnesses the signing of the marriage license.
- Keeps bride on schedule.
- Dances with best man during the bridal party dance.
- Helps bride change into her going away clothes.
- Mails wedding announcements after the wedding.
- Returns bridal slip, if rented.

BEST MAN

- Responsible for organizing ushers' activities.
- Organizes bachelor party for groom.
- Drives groom to ceremony site and sees that he is properly dressed before the wedding.
- Arrives dressed at ceremony site 1 hour before the wedding for photographs.
- Brings marriage license to wedding.
- Pays the clergyman, musicians, photographer, and any other service providers the day of the wedding.
- Holds the bride's ring for the groom, if no ring bearer, until needed by officiant.
- Witnesses the signing of the marriage license.
- Drives newlyweds to reception if no hired driver.
- Offers first toast at reception, usually before dinner.
- Keeps groom on schedule.
- Dances with maid of honor during the bridal party dance.
- May drive couple to airport or honeymoon suite.
- Oversees return of tuxedo rentals for groom and ushers, on time and in good condition.

RIDESMAIDS

- Assist maid/matron of honor in planning bridal shower.
- Assist bride with errands and addressing invitations.
- Participate in all pre-wedding parties.
- Arrive at dressing site 2 hours before ceremony.
- Arrive dressed at ceremony site 1 hour before the wedding for photographs.
- Walk behind ushers in order of height during the processional, either in pairs or in single file.
- Sit next to ushers at the head table.
- Dance with ushers and other important guests.
- Encourage single women to participate in the bouquet-tossing ceremony.

*U*SHERS

- Help best man with bachelor party.
- Arrive dressed at ceremony site 1 hour before the wedding for photographs.
- Distribute wedding programs and maps to the reception as guests arrive.
- Seat guests at the ceremony as follows:
    - -- If female, offer the right arm.
    - -- If male, walk along his left side.
    - -- If couple, offer right arm to female; male follows a step or two behind.
    - -- Seat bride's guests in left pews.
    - -- Seat groom's guests in right pews.
    - -- Maintain equal number of guests in left and right pews, if possible.
    - -- Should a group of guests arrive at the same time, seat the eldest woman first.
    - -- Just prior to the processional, escort groom's mother to her seat; then escort bride's mother to her seat.
- Two ushers may roll carpet down the aisle after both mothers are seated.
- If pew ribbons are used, two ushers may loosen them one row at a time after the ceremony.
- Direct guests to the reception site.
- Dance with bridesmaids and other important guests.

Bride's Mother

- Helps prepare guest list for bride and her family.
- Helps plan the wedding ceremony and reception.
- Helps bride select her bridal gown.
- Helps bride keep track of gifts received.
- Selects her own attire according to the formality and color of the wedding.
- Makes accommodations for bride's out of town guests.
- Arrives dressed at ceremony site 1 hour before the wedding for photographs.
- Is the last person to be seated right before the processional begins.
- Sits in the left front pew to the left of bride's father during the ceremony.
- May stand up to signal the start of the processional.
- Can witness the signing of the marriage license.
- Dances with the groom after the first dance.
- Acts as hostess at the reception.

BRIDE'S FATHER

- Helps prepare guest list for bride and her family.
- Selects attire that complements groom's attire.
- Rides to the ceremony with bride in limousine.
- Arrives dressed at ceremony site 1 hour before the wedding for photographs.
- After giving bride away, sits in the left front pew to the right of bride's mother. If divorced, sits in second or third row unless financing the wedding.
- When officiant asks, "Who gives this bride away?" answers, "Her mother and I do" or something similar.
- Can witness the signing of the marriage license.
- Dances with bride after first dance.
- Acts as host at the reception.

*G*ROOM'S *M*OTHER

- Helps prepare guest list for groom and his family.
- Selects attire that complements mother of the bride's attire.
- Makes accommodations for groom's out-of-town guests.
- With groom's father, plans rehearsal dinner.
- Arrives dressed at ceremony site 1 hour before the wedding for photographs.
- May stand up to signal the start of the processional.
- Can witness the signing of the marriage license.

GROOM'S FATHER

- Helps prepare guest list for groom and his family.
- Selects attire that complements groom's attire.
- With groom's mother, plans rehearsal dinner.
- Offers toast to bride at rehearsal dinner.
- Arrives dressed at ceremony site 1 hour before the wedding for photographs.
- Can witness the signing of the marriage license.

FLOWER GIRL

- Usually between the ages of four and eight.
- Attends rehearsal to practice her role but is not required to attend pre-wedding parties.
- Arrives dressed at ceremony site 45 minutes before the wedding for photographs.
- Carries a basket filled with loose rose petals to strew along bride's path during processional, if allowed by ceremony site.
- If very young, may sit with her parents during ceremony.

RING BEARER

- Usually between the ages of four and eight.
- Attends rehearsal to practice his role but is not required to attend pre-wedding parties.
- Arrives at ceremony site 45 minutes before the wedding for photographs.
- Carries a white pillow with rings attached.
- If younger than 7 years, carries artificial rings.
- If very young, may sit with his parents during ceremony.
- After the ceremony, carries ring pillow upside down so artificial rings will not show.

*P*ERSONAL *N*OTES

WHO PAYS FOR WHAT

Bride and/or Bride's Family

- Engagement party
- Wedding consultant's fee
- Bridal gown, veil and accessories
- Wedding stationery, calligraphy and postage
- Wedding gift for bridal couple
- Groom's wedding ring
- Gifts for bridesmaids
- Bridesmaids' bouquets
- Pre-wedding parties and bridesmaids' luncheon
- Photography and videography
- Bride's medical exam and blood test
- Wedding guest book and other accessories
- Total cost of the ceremony, including location, flowers, music, rental items and accessories
- Total cost of the reception, including location, flowers, music, rental items, accessories, food, beverages, cake, decorations, favors, etc.
- Transportation for bridal party to ceremony and reception
- Own attire and travel expenses

Groom and/or Groom's Family

- Own travel expenses and attire
- Rehearsal dinner
- Wedding gift for bridal couple
- Bride's wedding ring
- Gifts for groom's attendants
- Medical exam for groom including blood test
- Bride's bouquet and going away corsage
- Mothers' and grandmothers' corsages
- All boutonnieres
- Officiant's fee
- Marriage license
- Honeymoon expenses

Attendants

- Own attire except flowers
- Travel expenses
- Bridal shower paid for by maid of honor and bridesmaids
- Bachelor party paid for by best man and ushers

WEDDING FORMATIONS

The following section illustrates the typical ceremony formations (processional, recessional and altar line up) for both Christian and Jewish weddings, as well as the typical formations for the receiving line, head table, and parents' tables at the reception.

These ceremony formations are included in the *Wedding Party Responsibility Cards,* published by Wedding Solutions Publishing, Inc.. This attractive set of cards makes it very easy for your wedding party to remember their place in these formations. Give one card to each member of your wedding party... they will appreciate it.

The *Wedding Party Responsibility Cards* are available at most major bookstores or can be ordered on-line at *www.yourbridalsuperstore.com.*

CHRISTIAN CEREMONY

ALTAR LINE UP

Bride's Pews   Groom's Pews

ABBREVIATIONS

B = Bride   GF = Groom's Father
G = Groom   GM = Groom's Mother
BM = Best Man   BMa = Bridesmaids
MH = Maid of Honor   U = Ushers
BF = Bride's Father   FG = Flower Girl
BMo = Bride's Mother   RB = Ring Bearer
                             O = Officiant

*C*HRISTIAN *C*EREMONY

*P*ROCESSIONAL   *R*ECESSIONAL

ABBREVIATIONS

B = Bride
G = Groom
BM = Best Man
MH = Maid of Honor
BF = Bride's Father
BMo = Bride's Mother

GF = Groom's Father
GM = Groom's Mother
BMa = Bridesmaids
U = Ushers
FG = Flower Girl
RB = Ring Bearer
O = Officiant

*J*EWISH *C*EREMONY

*A*LTAR *L*INE *U*P

Groom's Pews	Bride's Pews

ABBREVIATIONS

B = Bride
G = Groom
BM = Best Man
MH = Maid of Honor
BF = Bride's Father
BMo = Bride's Mother

GF = Groom's Father
GM = Groom's Mother
BMa = Bridesmaids
U = Ushers
FG = Flower Girl
RB = Ring Bearer
R = Rabbi

JEWISH CEREMONY

PROCESSIONAL

RECESSIONAL

ABBREVIATIONS

B = Bride	GF = Groom's Father
G = Groom	GM = Groom's Mother
BM = Best Man	BMa = Bridesmaids
MH = Maid of Honor	U = Ushers
BF = Bride's Father	FG = Flower Girl
BMo = Bride's Mother	RB = Ring Bearer
	R = Rabbi

Receiving Line

Head Table

Parents' Table

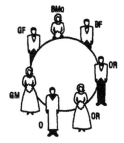

Abbreviations

B = Bride	GF = Groom's Father
G = Groom	GM = Groom's Mother
BM = Best Man	BMa = Bridesmaids
MH = Maid of Honor	U = Ushers
BF = Bride's Father	OR = Other Relatives
BMo = Bride's Mother	O = Officiant

THINGS TO BRING

TO THE REHEARSAL

Bride's List:

- Wedding announcements (for maid of honor to mail after the wedding)
- Bridesmaids' gifts (if not already given)
- Camera and film
- Fake bouquet or ribbon bouquet from bridal shower
- Groom's gift (if not already given)
- Reception maps and wedding programs
- Rehearsal information and ceremony formations
- Flower girl basket and ring bearer pillow
- Seating diagrams for head table and parents' tables
- Wedding schedule of events/timeline
- Tape player with wedding music

Groom's List:

- Bride's gift (if not already given)
- Marriage license
- Ushers' gifts (if not already given)
- Service providers' fees to give to best man or wedding consultant so s/he can pay them at the wedding

TO THE CEREMONY

Bride's List:

- Aspirin/Alka Seltzer
- Bobby pins
- Breath spray/mints
- Bridal gown
- Bridal gown box
- Cake knife
- Change of clothes for going away
- Clear nail polish
- Deodorant
- Garter
- Gloves
- Groom's ring
- Guest book
- Hair brush
- Hair spray
- Head piece
- Iron
- Jewelry
- Kleenex
- Lint brush
- Luggage
- Make-up
- Mirror
- Nail polish
- Panty hose
- Passport
- Perfume
- Personal camera
- Plume pen for guest book

- Powder
- Purse
- Safety pins
- Scotch tape/masking tape
- Sewing kit
- Shoes
- Something old
- Something new
- Something borrowed
- Something blue
- Spot remover
- Straight pins
- Tampons or sanitary napkins
- Toasting goblets
- Toothbrush & paste

Groom's List:

- Airline tickets
- Announcements
- Aspirin/Alka Seltzer
- Breath spray/mints
- Bride's ring
- Change of clothes for going away
- Cologne
- Cuff Links
- Cummerbund
- Deodorant
- Hair comb
- Hair spray
- Kleenex
- Lint brush
- Luggage
- Neck tie
- Passport
- Shirt
- Shoes
- Socks
- Toothbrush & paste
- Tuxedo
- Underwear

*P*AYMENT TRACKING
CHART

Ceremony Site	Contract Date	Total Cost
Deposit/Date	Next Pay/Date	Final Pay/Date

Clergy Services	Contract Date	Total Cost
Deposit/Date	Next Pay/Date	Final Pay/Date

Reception Site	Contract Date	Total Cost
Deposit/Date	Next Pay/Date	Final Pay/Date

Caterer	Contract Date	Total Cost
Deposit/Date	Next Pay/Date	Final Pay/Date

*P*AYMENT TRACKING CHART

Photographer	Contract Date	Total Cost
Deposit/Date	Next Pay/Date	Final Pay/Date

Videographer	Contract Date	Total Cost
Deposit/Date	Next Pay/Date	Final Pay/Date

Music (Cerem.)	Contract Date	Total Cost
Deposit/Date	Next Pay/Date	Final Pay/Date

Music (Recep.)	Contract Date	Total Cost
Deposit/Date	Next Pay/Date	Final Pay/Date

PAYMENT TRACKING CHART

Florist	Contract Date	Total Cost
Deposit/Date	Next Pay/Date	Final Pay/Date

Bridal Boutique	Contract Date	Total Cost
Deposit/Date	Next Pay/Date	Final Pay/Date

Stationery	Contract Date	Total Cost
Deposit/Date	Next Pay/Date	Final Pay/Date

Decorations	Contract Date	Total Cost
Deposit/Date	Next Pay/Date	Final Pay/Date

PAYMENT TRACKING

CHART

Limousine	Contract Date	Total Cost
Deposit/Date	Next Pay/Date	Final Pay/Date

Tuxedo Rental	Contract Date	Total Cost
Deposit/Date	Next Pay/Date	Final Pay/Date

Bakery	Contract Date	Total Cost
Deposit/Date	Next Pay/Date	Final Pay/Date

Rental Items	Contract Date	Total Cost
Deposit/Date	Next Pay/Date	Final Pay/Date

ASY

HONEYMOON

LANNING

A comprehensive guide
containing all the information
a bride and groom
should know when
planning a Honeymoon.

𝒞ONTENTS

Types of

Honeymoons

Listed on the following pages are sample honeymoon plans -- both traditional and less traditional. A brief description of some of the most popular honeymoon trips (ones that have remained popular with newlyweds for generations) is provided as well.

You can get very helpful information on planning a vacation package in the following brochures:

United States Tour Operator Association
(212) 750-7371
* *How to Select a Tour Vacation Package*
* *Worldwide Tour and Vacation Package Finder*
* *The Standard for Confident Travel*

Traditional

Honeymoons

CRUISES

Cruises are a popular retreat for those who want the luxury of a hospitable resort with the added benefit of visiting one or more new areas. There are hundreds of different cruise options available to you. Typically, almost everything is included in the cost of your cruise: extravagant dining, unlimited group and individual activities, relaxing days and lively nights.

Costs vary greatly depending on the location the cruise will visit (if any) and your cabin accommodations. Locations range from traveling the Mississippi River to encircling the Greek Isles. Spend some time choosing your cabin. Most of them are small, but pay attention to distracting things, such as noisy areas and busy pathways, that might be located close by.

Even though most everything is included in your cost, be sure to ask about those items which may not be included. Request a helpful publication entitled *Answers to Your Most Frequently Asked Questions*, published by Cruise Lines International Association, (212) 921-0066.

ALL INCLUSIVE RESORTS

Many newlyweds, tired from the previous months of wedding planning and accompanying stress, opt for the worry-free guarantee of an all-inclusive resort. Some resorts are for the entire family, some are for couples only (not necessarily newlywed), and some are strictly for honeymooners. Most of these resorts are nestled on a picturesque island beach catering to your relaxation needs.

Most offer numerous sports, water activities, entertainment, and exceptional service and attention. Your costs will vary depending on the location you choose, and there are many, many to choose from. "All-inclusive" means everything is included in your price. You won't have to worry about meals, drinks, tour fees or even tips.

One way of considering if this is a good option for you is to list all of the activities that the vacation package offers that you are interested in. Add up the individual costs and compare. If you wouldn't be participating much in the activities, food, and drink, you may actually save money by arranging your own trip at an independent resort. Even still, many couples prefer to spend the extra money in exchange for a vacation free of planning and wearying decisions.

Because of its convenience, many couples choose this resort option as the setting for their honeymoon. Some of the most popular all-inclusive resorts are Club Med and Sandals.

THE POCONOS

The Poconos Honeymoon resorts are located in Pennsylvania and are considered to be some of the most popular Honeymoon destinations around. The Poconos offer a variety of individual resorts, each heavily laden with fanciful symbols of romance and sweet desires. The atmosphere is perfect for those who want to be enveloped in a surrounding where you'll never forget you're in love and on your honeymoon. Some travel packages here are considered all-inclusive, but as always, be sure to ask about exclusions and extras.

Poconos tourism information:
    1-800-POCONOS

WALT DISNEY WORLD

Another popular destination for those seeking a "theme" resort are those offered as *Disney's Fairy Tale Honeymoons*. These vacation packages include accommodations at Disney's exclusive resorts and admission to their theme parks. Some packages are also available with accommodations at some of the privately owned resorts at Disney World. Prices for Disney packages can range greatly depending on your tastes and the amount of activity you desire. For information about Disney's honeymoon packages, call (407) 828-3400.

Inquire with your travel agent about day or overnight cruises leaving from nearby ports in Florida. This is one way to combine two very popular honeymoon options into one!

Other popular and traditional honeymoon plans are as follows:

- Enjoying the beaches and unique treasures of the Hawaiian islands

- Exploring Northern California's romantic wine country

- Ski and snowboard package getaways in Vermont, New Hampshire, Colorado, and Northern California

- Camping and hiking within the beautiful and adventurous National Parks

- Sightseeing, touring, and exploring a variety of points in Europe via the rail system

- Island hopping on a cruise ship around the Greek Isles

- Enjoying a fanciful and adventurous journey on the Orient Express

Less Traditional Honeymoons

- Bicycling in Nova Scotia while relaxing at quaint Bed and Breakfast Inns

- Participating in a white water river rafting expedition in Oregon

- Mingling with the owners and fellow guests on an Old West Dude Ranch

- Visiting landmarks and parks while enjoying the convenience of a traveling home in a rented RV

- Mustering up the courage and stamina for an aggressive hiking tour of the Canadian Rockies

- Training for and participating in a dog sled race in the brisk tundra of Alaska

- "Roughing it" while enjoying the splendor of a safari in East Africa

CHOOSING YOUR DESTINATION

Maybe your idea of a perfect honeymoon is 10 days of resting in a beach chair and romantic strolls in the evening; but for your fiancé, it may be 10 days of adventure and discovery. The choices for honeymoon vacations are as varied as the bride and groom themselves. Deciding together on a honeymoon destination is a wonderful opportunity to discover more about each other and negotiate a vacation that will leave both of you relaxed, fulfilled, and even more in love.

First, determine the type of atmosphere and climate you prefer. Then consider the types of activities you would like to engage in.

Do you want the weather to be hot for swimming at the beach... or warm for long guided tours of unknown cities... or cooler for day-long hikes in the woods... or cold for optimum skiing conditions? Keep in mind the time of year in which your wedding falls. Will you be escaping from warm or cool temperatures?

If you have a specific destination in mind, you (or your travel agent) will need to do some research to be sure the weather conditions will be suitable for your planned activities.

Review the previous chapters on traditional and non-traditional honeymoons and note what you feel are the pros and cons of each type of vacation. The two of you should have lots of images and possibilities in your mind at this point! The next step is to determine the most perfect atmosphere to provide the setting for your honeymoon. The following sections, *Creating A Wish List* and *Helpful Resources*, will guide you through this next step and beyond.

CREATING A
WISH LIST

Together with your fiancé, complete the following wish list worksheet. You should each check off your preferences even if both of you don't agree on them. There are many locations that provide a variety of activities. Remember, you don't need to spend every minute of your honeymoon together, but your honeymoon destination should be one that intrigues both of you.

This worksheet is divided into 5 sections. You will be considering location, accommodations, meals, activities, and night life.

While responding to the following, be as true to your interests as possible; don't concern yourself with finances and practicality at this point. This is your chance to let your mind wander! Think about what you would like to fill your days and nights with. This is the honeymoon of your dreams...

You step out of the plane, train, car or boat that took you to your honeymoon destination. You sigh with satisfaction at the memory of your flawless and enjoyable wedding as your feet touch the ground.

What type of overall atmosphere do you see yourself stepping into?

What is the weather like?

Do you picture a long stretch of beach, towering mountains, blossoming vineyards, or city skyscrapers? Is the dry sand of the desert blowing around or is everything captured under glistening snowcaps?

Are there many people walking around (many locals, many tourists), or is it a secluded retreat?

Are you relaxing indoors in a resort with a pampering environment that caters to your comfort? Do you return to a simple, modest hotel or motel after a long day of sightseeing, touring, and dining? Are you camping in the middle of your activities --hiking, climbing, fishing, etc.?

Do you see yourself interacting much with others? Would you like to have these activities be organized? Are there vistas and horizons to gaze endlessly upon, or is there an abundance of visual activity and changing scenery?

Are you enjoying exotic foods elaborately displayed and available to you at your leisure? Are you testing out your sense of adventure on the local cuisine and dining hot spots? Are you eating fast foods and pizza in exchange for spending your time and money on other items and activities that make your vacation exciting?

Are your evenings filled with romantic strolls or festivities that run late into the night? Are you staying in for romantic evenings or re-energizing for another busy day of honeymooning?

HOW TO USE THIS WORKSHEET:

Each of you separately should place a check mark next to the items or images on the wish list that appeal to you. After you have finished, highlight those items that both of you feel are important (the items that were checked by both of you).

Then each of you should highlight, in a different colored marker or pen, 2-3 items in each category that you feel are very important to you (even though the other person may not have checked it off.)

$\mathscr{B}$ = BRIDE $\mathscr{G}$ = GROOM	$\mathscr{B}$ ✓	$\mathscr{G}$ ✓
Location:		
hot weather		
mild weather		
cold weather		
dry climate		
moist climate		
sand and beaches		
lakes/ponds		
wilderness/wooded areas		
mountains		
fields		
city streets		
small local town		
large metropolitan area		
popular tourist destination		
visiting among the locals		
nighttime weather conducive to outdoor activities		
nighttime weather conducive to indoor activities		

$\mathscr{B}$ = BRIDE $\mathscr{G}$ = GROOM	$\mathscr{B}$ ✓	$\mathscr{G}$ ✓
"modern" resources and service available		
"roughing it" on your own		
culture and customs you are familiar and comfortable with		
new cultures and customs you would like to get to know		
Accommodations:		
part of a larger resort community		
a stand alone building		
lodging amongst other fellow tourists		
lodging amongst couples only		
lodging amongst fellow newlyweds only		
lodging amongst locals		
large room or suite		
plush, highly decorated surroundings		
modestly sized room		
modest decor		

$\mathscr{B}$ = BRIDE $\mathscr{G}$ = GROOM	$\mathscr{B}$ ✓	$\mathscr{G}$ ✓
balcony		
private Jacuzzi in room		
room service		
chamber maid service		
laundry service available		
laundry room available		
beauty salon on premises		
workout gym on premises		
gift shop on premises		
pool on premises		
poolside bar service		
sauna, hot tub on premises		
common gathering lounge for guests		
Meals:		
casual dining		
formal dining		
prepared by executive chefs		
prepared by yourself/grocery store		

B = BRIDE G = GROOM	B ✓	G ✓
variety of local and regional estaurants		
traditional "American" cuisine		
opportunity for picnics		
exotic, international menu		
formal dining		
entertainment while dining		
planned meal times		
dining based on your own schedule		
fast food restaurants		
vegetarian meals		
special diet meals		
delis		
diners		
Activities:		
sun bathing		
snorkeling		
diving		

$\mathcal{B}$ = BRIDE $\quad$ $\mathcal{G}$ = GROOM	$\mathcal{B}$ ✓	$\mathcal{G}$ ✓
swimming		
jet skiing		
water skiing		
fishing		
sailing		
snow skiing		
snow boarding		
hiking		
camping		
rock climbing		
golf		
tennis		
aerobics		
site-seeing suggestions and guidance		
planned bus/guided tours		
ability to go off on your own		
historic tours		
art museums		
theater		
exploring family heritage		

$\mathcal{B}$ = BRIDE $\mathcal{G}$ = GROOM	$\mathcal{B}$ ✓	$\mathcal{G}$ ✓
Night Life:		
quiet strolls		
outdoor activities		
sitting and relaxing outdoors		
sitting and relaxing in front of a fireplace		
being alone with each other		
being out with the locals		
being out with other newlyweds		
discovering new cultures and forms of entertainment		
dancing		
visiting bars/pubs		
theater/shows		
gambling		

B = BRIDE *G* = GROOM	*B* ✓	*G* ✓
Other important elements:		

Your wish lists, at this point, probably look like a list of *all* of the positive elements of *all* of your dream vacations combined. List as many things as you can think of. The more information you have, the better the suggestions your travel agent (or yourself if you'll be doing your own research) will be able to make.

Together, using this wish list, you will discover a honeymoon destination and match a honeymoon style that will fulfill your dreams.

The resource leads and exercises provided in the rest of this book will help you get from wish list to reality. Happy planning!

Personal Notes

HELPFUL RESOURCES

Now that you have a completed wish list, take this list to your travel agent. If you don't already have a travel agent, use the following section for help in selecting a reputable agent.

A good travel agent, especially one who works with a lot of honeymooners, will be able to tell you about several different places that match your wish list while staying within your budget. (The section entitled *Creating A Budget* will prove invaluable in determining exactly what your budget will be). Your travel agent should be able to provide a variety of options which contain different combinations of the elements of your wish list. Discuss with him/her which "lower priority" items you are willing to forego in order to experience the best of your "top priorities."

TRAVEL AGENTS

Hiring the services of a good travel agent will take a lot of unnecessary pressure off of you. In the past, you may have felt that you did not need the assistance of a travel agent when planning a vacation. Planning a honeymoon, however, can often be far more involved and stressful than a "regular" vacation, due to the simple fact that you are also deeply enmeshed in the planning of your wedding!

Therefore, you should take advantage of the professional resources available to you when working out the small details and finding the best values. Keep in mind, though, that you will still probably want to do some research on your own, ask for second opinions, and, most of all, read the fine print.

Since a travel agent can become one of your most valuable resources, you will want to consider a few important things when trying to select one:

Ask family, friends, and coworkers for personal recommendations (especially from former honeymooners).

If you are unable to find an agent through a personal referral, then select a few agencies that are established nearby (from newspapers, phone books, etc.)

Next, you will want to make an appointment with an agent or speak to one over the phone. Pay close attention to the following and then make your decision.

Find out if they are a member of the *American Society of Travel Agents* (ASTA). Additionally, find out if they are also a *Certified Travel Counselor* (CTC), or possibly a *Destination Specialist* (DS).

ASTA: Members of this organization are required to have at least 5 years travel agent experience. They also agree to adhere to strict codes and standards of integrity in travel issues as established by the national society. In most states, there are no formal regulations requiring certain qualifications for being a travel agent. In other words, any person can decide to call him/herself, and thus advertise as, a travel agent.

CTC: Certified Travel Counselors have successfully completed a 2 year program in travel management.

DS: Destination Specialists have successfully completed studies focusing on a particular region.

For a list of ASTA agencies in your area, call or write:

> **American Society of Travel Agents**
> **Consumer Affairs Department**
> **1101 King Street, Suite 200**
> **Alexandria, VA 22314**
> **(703) 739-8739**

A listing for the local chapter in your area can also be found in your local phone book or visit their web site at **www.astanet.com**.

For a list of Destination Specialists and Certified Travel Agents in your area, call or write:

> **Institute of Certified Travel Agents**
> **148 Linden Street**
> **P.O. Box 56**
> **Wellesley, MA 02181**
> **(800) 542-4282**
> **(press "0" to be connected to a Travel Counselor)**

Questions to Qualify Your Travel Agent

How long has the Travel Agency been in business?

How long has the Travel Agent been with the agency?

How much experience does the Travel Agent have? Any special studies or travels?

Do they have a good resource library?

Does the agent/agency have a variety of brochures to offer?

Do they have video tapes to lend?

Do they have a recommended reading list of travel aid books?

Does the agent seem to understand your responses on your wish list and budget?

Does he/she seem excited to help you?

Does the agent listen carefully to your ideas? Take notes on your conversations? Ask you questions to ensure a full understanding?

Is the agent able to offer a variety of different possibilities that suit your interests based on your wish list? Do the suggestions fall within your budget?

Can the agent relay back to you (in his/her own words) what your wish list priorities are? What your budget priorities are?

Is the agent prompt in getting back in touch with you?

Is the agent reasonably quick in coming up with suggestions and alternatives? Are the suggestions exciting and within reason?

Does the agent take notes on your interests (degree of sports, leisure, food, etc.)?

Does the travel agency provide a 24 hour emergency help line?

Are you documenting your conversations and getting all of your travel plans and reservations confirmed in writing?

Aside from just offering information and arrangements about locations and discounts, a good travel agent should also provide you with information about passports, customs, travel and health insurance, travelers' checks, and any other information important to a traveler.

OTHER SOURCES

National bridal magazines and general travel magazines are a great place to search for honeymoon ideas. But remember, you cannot always believe every word in paid advertising.

In addition to the information your travel agent provides, you can also attain maps, brochures, and other useful items on your own. At the end of this section, you will find many useful phone numbers to help you in contacting tourist bureaus and travel agencies worldwide. These offices are extremely helpful in acquiring both general information (information about the weather, tourist attractions, landmarks, and even coupons or promotional brochures "selling" the area) and more specific information about reputable hotels, inns, bed and breakfasts, restaurants, etc.

Also provided in this section are phone numbers for sources specializing in information about traveling by train (in the United States as well as abroad) and for camping and hiking throughout the country.

Your local library, the travel section of book stores, and travel stores are also excellent sources for finding information and tips relevant to your travel needs. You will find books on traveling in general as well as books specific to the region or destination you will be visiting. There are numerous tour books, maps, language books and tapes, as well as books about a location's culture, traditions, customs, climate, and geography.

These books are a great source of information since they are independent from the locations they describe and are therefore impartial, objective, and usually contain correct, unbiased information. You can also find books and other resources describing (and sometimes rating) restaurants, hotels, shows, and tours. Books on bargain hunting and finding the best deals are common as well.

SOURCES TO READ

The Traveler's Reading Guide: Ready-Made Reading Lists for the Armchair Traveler, by Maggy Simone
A comprehensive listing of varied travel resources for almost every place in the world.

The Stephen Birnbaum Travel Guides

Frommer's Guides

Michelin's Green Guides

Michelin's Red Guides

Insight Guides

Let's Go! guides

Fodor's Guides

Fielding Travel Books

AYH Handbook and Hosteler's Manual: Europe

AYH Handbook and Hosteler's Manual: United States

The New York Times Practical Traveler

Mobil Travel Guide

Background Notes
> *U.S. Government notes containing information about the culture, people, geography, history, government, economy, and maps of most countries worldwide.*
> The U.S. Government Printing Office Cost: $1.00
> (1-202-512-1800)
> or download at: www.access.gpo.gov

101 Tips For Adventure Travelers
> Overseas Adventure Travel
> (1-800-221-0814)

National Park Service publications:
> (1-202-208-4747)
> www.nps.gov
> • *National Park System Map and Guide*
> • *The National Parks: Index*

National Forest Service publications:
> (1-202-205-1760)
> *A Guide to Your National Forests*

The Internet
If you have Internet access you can acquire volumes and volumes of information (and titillating pictures) about your destination or even "chat" with other soon-to-be honeymooners. If you don't currently have access, local libraries often provide limited free time and user-assistance for their members.

SOURCES TO CALL

State Tourism Bureaus

Alabama Bureau of Tourism
　　800-ALABAMA
Alaska Division of Tourism
　　907-465-2010
Arizona Office of Tourism
　　800-842-8257
Arkansas Dept. of Parks and Tourism
　　800-NATURAL
California Tourism Office
　　800-862-2543
Colorado Tourism Board
　　800-COLORADO
Connecticut Tourism Division
　　800-CT-BOUND
D.C. Convention and Visitors Association
　　202-789-7000
Delaware Tourism Office
　　800-441-8846
Florida Division of Tourism
　　904-938-2981
Georgia Department of Industry & Trade
　　800-VISIT-GA
Hawaii Visitors Bureau
　　800-VISIT-HI
Idaho Travel Council
　　800-635-7820
Illinois Travel Information Center
　　800-487-2446

Indiana Department of Commerce
    800-289-6646
Iowa Development Commission
    800-345-IOWA
Kansas Department of Travel & Tourism
    800-2-KANSAS
Kentucky Dept. of Travel Development
    800-225-TRIP
Louisiana Office of Tourism
    800-33-GUMBO
Maine Publicity Bureau
    800-782-6496
Maryland Office of Tourist Development
    800-543-1036
Massachusetts Department of Tourism
    800-447-MASS
Michigan Department of Commerce
    800-5432-YES
Minnesota Office of Tourism
    800-657-3700
Mississippi Office of Tourism
    800-WARMEST
Missouri Division of Tourism
    800-877-1234
Montana Travel Promotion Division
    800-VISIT-MT
Nebraska Dept. of Travel and Tourism
    800-228-4307
Nevada Commission on Tourism
    800-NEVADA-8
New Hampshire Dept. of Vacation Travel
    800-386-4664

New Jersey Office of Travel & Tourism
800-JERSEY-7
New Mexico Tourism & Travel
800-545-2040
New York Division of Tourism
New York State: 800-CALL-NYS
New York City: 800-NYC-VISIT
North Carolina Travel & Tourism Div.
800-VISIT-NC
North Dakota Tourism Division
800-HELLO-ND
Ohio Department of Travel & Tourism
800-BUCKEYE
Oklahoma Tourism and Recreation Dept.
800-652-6552
Oregon Division of Tourism
800-547-7842
Pennsylvania Department of Tourism
800-VISIT-PA
Poconos: 800-POCONOS
Rhode Island Tourism Division
800-556-2484
South Carolina Department of Parks,
Recreation, and Tourism
800-346-3634
South Dakota Division of Tourism
800-S-DAKOTA
Tennessee Department of Tourism
800-836-6200
Texas Travel and Information Bureau
800-888-8-TEX
Utah Travel Council
800-200-1160

Vermont Travel Division
    800-VERMONT
Virginia Division of Tourism
    800-VISIT-VA
Washington Tourism Development
    800-544-1800
West Virginia Div. of Tourism & Parks
    800-CALL-WVA
Wisconsin Division of Tourism
    800-432-TRIP
Wyoming Division of Tourism
    800-CALL-WYO
U.S. Virgin Islands Division of Tourism
    800-USVI-INFO

International Tourism Bureaus

Anguilla Tourist Information
    516-271-2600
Antigua Tourist Office
    212-541-4117
Argentina Tourist Information
    800-722-5737
Aruba Tourism Authority
    201-330-0800
Australian Tourist Commission
    800-445-4400
Austrian National Tourist Office
    213-477-3332
Bahamas Tourist Office
    800-422-4262

Balkan Holidays
212-573-5330
Barbados Board of Tourism
212-986-6516
Belgian Tourist Office
212-758-8130
Belize Tourist Board
800-624-0686
Bermuda Department of Tourism
800-223-6106
Bonaire Tourist Information Office
212-956-5911
Brazil Tourism Office
212-759-7878
British Tourist Office
800-462-2748
Canadian Consulate
213-687-7432
Alberta: 800-661-8888
British Columbia: 800-663-6000
Manitoba: 800-665-0040
New Brunswick: 800-561-0123
Newfoundland: 800-563-6353
Nova Scotia: 800-341-6096
Ontario: 800-ONTARIO
Prince Edward: 800-566-0267
Quebec: 800-363-7777
Saskatchewan: 800-363-7777
Yukon: 403-667-5340
Caribbean Tourism Organization
212-682-0435
Cayman Islands Department of Tourism
213-738-1968

Chile National Tourist Board
800-825-2332
China National Tourist Office
818-545-7505
Colombian Consulate
202-332-7476
Cook Islands Tourist Authority
800-624-6250
Costa Rican Tourist Board
800-343-6332
Curacao Tourist Board
212-683-7660
Cyprus Consulate General
212-686-6016
CEDOK (Czech Republic and Slovakia)
212-689-9720
Denmark Tourist Board
212-949-2333
Dominican Republic Tourist Info. Center
212-575-4966
Egyptian Tourist Authority
415-781-7676
Fiji Visitors Bureau
310-568-1616
Finland Tourist Board
212-949-2333
French Government Tourist Office
212-757-1125
French West Indies (St. Martin, Martinique, Guadeloupe)
212-757-1125
German National Tourist Office
800-462-2748

Greece National Tourist Authority
212-421-5777
Grenada Department of Tourism
212-687-9554
Guam Visitors Bureau
800-US3-GUAM
Guatemala Tourist Commission
800-742-4529
Honduras Tourist Bureau
213-682-3377
Hong Kong Tourist Association
212-869-5008
Hungary Tourist Board
201-592-8585
Iceland Tourist Board
212-949-2333
India Tourist Office
212-586-4901
Indonesian Tourist Office
213-387-2078
Ireland Tourist Board
800-223-6470
Israeli Government Tourist Office
212-560-0621
Italian Tourist Office
310-820-0098
Jamaican Tourist Board
800-327-9857
Japan National Tourist Office
415-989-7140
Kenya Tourist Office
212-486-1300

Korea National Tourist Office
      213-623-1226
Luxembourg National Tourist Office
      212-370-9850
Macau Tourist Office
      213-851-3402 OR 800-331-7150
Malaysian Tourist Centre
      213-689-9702
Malta National Tourist Office
      212-213-6686
Mexican Tourist Office
      800-44-MEXICO
Monaco Government Tourist Office
      212-759-5227
Morocco National Tourist Office
      212-557-2520
Netherlands Board of Tourism
      212-557-2520
New Zealand Tourist Office
      800-388-5494
Norway Scandinavia Tourist Offices
      212-949-2333
Panama Tourist Bureau
      305-442-1892
Papua/New Guinea Tourist Office
      714-752-5440
Philippine Department of Tourism
      213-487-4525
Poland National Tourism Office
      212-338-9412
Portugal National Tourist Office
      212-354-4403

Puerto Rico Tourism Office
        212-599-6262
Romanian National Tourist Office
        212-697-6971
Russian Travel Information Office
        212-757-3884
Singapore Tourist Board
        212-302-4861
South African Tourism Board
        800-822-5368
Spain National Tourism Office
        212-759-8822
Sri Lanka Tourist Board
        202-483-4025
St. Kitts Tourist Board
        212-535-1234
St. Lucia Tourist Board
        212-867-2950
St. Maarten Tourist Office
        800-786-2278
St. Vincent/Grenadines Tourist Office
        212-687-4981
Sweden Travel & Tourism Board
        212-949-2333
Switzerland National Tourist Office
        212-757-5944
Tahitian Tourist Board
        212-207-1919
Taiwan Visitors Association
        212-466-0691
Thailand Tourism Authority
        213-382-2353

Trinidad and Tobago Tourist Board
        212-719-0540
Tunisian Tourist Office
        202-862-1850
Turkish Tourism Office
        212-687-2194
Venezuela Tourism Association
        800-331-0100

Other

National Park Service
        Office of Public Inquiries
        202-208-4747
        www.nps.gov
American Automobile Association;
        Travel Related Services Department
        407-444-8000
        www.aaa.com
Amtrak National Railroad Passenger Information
        800-872-7245
Rail Europe
        800-438-7245
Via Rail Canada
        800-304-4842

CREATING A BUDGET

You want your honeymoon to give you luxurious experiences and priceless memories. But you don't want to return from your vacation to be faced with debts and unnecessary feelings of guilt for not having stayed within a reasonable budget.

This should be the vacation of a lifetime. You can make this trip into anything your imagination allows. Pay attention to which experiences or details you would consider a "must have" and prioritize. As you work with your budget, stay focused on those top priority items and allow less "elaborate" solutions for lower priority items. If you stay true to your most important vacation objectives, the minor sacrifices along the way will barely be noticed.

Perhaps, at this point, you don't know how many days your honeymoon will last. Often, the number of days you'll vacation depends on the type of honeymoon you choose. If you (and your travel agent) are designing your own honeymoon, the typical cost-per-day will most likely determine your length of stay. If you opt for a cruise or another type of prearranged vacation, your length of stay will probably be dependent upon the designated length of the travel package. By determining a basic, overall budget at the start, you will know what your limits are.

Yes, this is a very romantic time... but try to remain realistic! Once you have an idea of your spending limits, your choices will be much easier to make.

Don't be discouraged if you're unable to spend an infinite amount of money on this trip. Very few couples are able to live life so carefree. You can still experience a honeymoon that will leave you filled with those priceless memories... it's all in the planning!

The following budget worksheets will help guide you in creating your honeymoon budget. You may want to make copies of this worksheet so that you can create several budget plans. Keep trying different variations until you are satisfied with how your expenses will be allocated. When comparing your potential honeymoon options, you'll find that laying out a simple budget is an effective, and essential, tool for making decisions.

GENERAL BUDGET

Traditionally the groom is responsible for the honeymoon. The groom will take on the challenges of gathering information and working through the necessary details of providing a perfect honeymoon for his new bride... and himself! Nowadays, many couples find it necessary for both the bride and groom to contribute to the cost in order to experience the honeymoon of their dreams. (*Today, the average newlywed couple spends $2,500-$3,500 on their honeymoon.*) Many couples, together, determine what each partner will contribute and then shape the budget from there.

Some couples find that including the suggestion of a "Money Contribution towards a Memorable Honeymoon" as a gift in their bridal registry is a great way for friends and family to contribute to the trip. Some couples also include some version of a "Dollar Dance" at their reception. This is a great way for the bride and groom to dance with many of their guests while accepting the dollar "dance fee" as a contribution to their honeymoon. Some couples choose to pursue less romantic options for building up the honeymoon savings... part time jobs, yard sales, etc..

Whatever your methods may be, remember that increasing the amount of money you will spend does not automatically ensure a more pleasurable and enjoyable vacation. Your most important and effective resource is your commitment to planning. You will see that, regardless of what your budget limits may be, your vacation possibilities are endless.

Note: Even if you think you have a good sense of what you will spend (or even if you plan on going with an all-inclusive package) going through this exercise is a smart way to ensure that there will be no surprises later on.

OVERALL BUDGET:

Amount from Wedding Budget set aside for Honeymoon:

$_____

Amount Groom is able to contribute from current funds/savings:

$_____

Amount Bride is able to contribute from current funds/savings:

$_____

Amount to be saved/acquired by Groom from now until the honeymoon date:
(monthly contributions, part-time job, gifts, bonuses)

$_____

Amount to be saved/acquired by Bride from now until the honeymoon date:
(monthly contributions, part-time job, gifts, bonuses)

$_____

OVERALL BUDGET AMOUNT:

$_____

Budget Notes

DETAILED BUDGET

BEFORE THE HONEYMOON:

Special honeymoon clothing purchases:

$\underline{\hspace{4cm}}$

Bride's trousseau (honeymoon lingerie):

$\underline{\hspace{4cm}}$

Sundries:
> (HELPFUL HINT: Make a list of what you already have and what you need to purchase. You can then use these lists as part of your Packing List. See *Packing Checklist.*)

$\underline{\hspace{4cm}}$

Film, disposable cameras, extra camera batteries:

$\underline{\hspace{4cm}}$

Maps, guide books, travel magazines:

$\underline{\hspace{4cm}}$

Foreign language books and tapes, translation dictionary:

$\underline{\hspace{4cm}}$

Passport photos, application fees:
> (See *International Travel*)

$\underline{\hspace{4cm}}$

Medical exam, inoculations:

    (See *International Travel*)

    $ _____

New blank journal:

    (IDEA: Create a beautiful *Honeymoon Memory Book* with a simple blank journal. Fill this journal with your thoughts, record of activities, mementos, phone numbers from new acquaintances, and travel notes from your honeymoon to enjoy and reminisce whenever you need an escape.)

    $ _____

Other items: _____

_____

    $ _____

> ### *BEFORE THE HONEYMOON* TOTAL AMOUNT:
>
> $ _____

***DURING THE HONEYMOON*:**

TRANSPORTATION

Airplane tickets:

$_____

Shuttle or cab (to and from airport):

$_____

Car rental :

$_____

Gasoline, tolls:

$_____

Taxis, buses, other public transportation:

$_____

Tips:

$_____

> *TRANSPORTATION*
> **TOTAL AMOUNT:**
>
> $_____

ACCOMMODATIONS

Hotel/resort room (total for entire stay):

$ _____

Room service:

$ _____

Miscellaneous "hidden costs":

Phone use, room taxes and surcharges, chambermaid and room service tips (see *Tipping Guide*), in-room liquor bar and snacks.

$ _____

ACCOMMODATIONS
TOTAL AMOUNT:

$ _____

MEALS

(NOTE: Don't forget to include the cost of drinks and gratuities in your meal estimates.)

Breakfast: $_____ *per meal*

x _____ *# days* = $_____

Lunch: $_____ *per meal*

x _____ *# days* = $_____

Casual Dinners: $_____ *per meal*

x _____ *# days* = $_____

Formal Dinners: $_____ *per meal*

x _____ *# days* = $_____

**Picnics, Snacks,
Temptations:** $_____ *per day*

x _____ *# days* = $_____

> ### *MEALS*
> ### TOTAL AMOUNT:
>
> $_____

ENTERTAINMENT

Sport and activity lessons (tennis, golf, ballroom dancing, etc.):

$ _____

Day excursions and tours (boat tours, diving, snorkeling, bus/guided tours, etc.):

$ _____

Shows, theater:

$ _____

Lounges, nightclubs, discos:
        (don't forget to include the cost of drinks and bar gratuities)

$ _____

Museum fees:

$ _____

Pampering (massages, spa treatments, hairdresser, etc.):

$ _____

ENTERTAINMENT
TOTAL AMOUNT:

$ _____

MISCELLANEOUS

Souvenirs for yourselves:

$_____

Souvenirs and gifts for family and friends:

$_____

Postcards (including cost of stamps):

$_____

Newspapers and magazines:

$_____

Additional film, replacement sundries, other:

$_____

MISCELLANEOUS
TOTAL AMOUNT:

$_____

AFTER THE HONEYMOON:

Film developing costs:

$_____

Photo Albums:

$_____

> ### *AFTER THE HONEYMOON* TOTAL AMOUNT:
>
> $_____

For All-Inclusive Resorts/Cruises and Travel Packages only:

Fill in the entire budget form above (simply put a "$0.00" on items to be included in the total package price), then list the total inclusive package price on the line below. Don't forget to include taxes and surcharges.

Inclusive Package Price:

$_____

> ### TOTAL BUDGET AMOUNT:
>
> $_____

Doing a budget analysis may be one of the most useful things you can do in planning your honeymoon. With all the options available, a good cost analysis will help make the most appropriate decisions very clear to you.

First, create a budget using the aforementioned worksheet for what you think allows for an ideal, yet reasonable, honeymoon. Highlight those expenses which are top priorities. For example, a spacious, ritzy hotel room may be the most important element for you. Or perhaps participating in numerous sports activities and excursions or enjoying fine dining is more important than a spacious room.

Next, as you come across different destinations and options that appeal to you, fill in a new budget worksheet. Compare the results to other potential trips. See how your priority items on each trip compare to one another. Determine the pros and cons of each. This is also an effective way of looking at the pros and cons of an all-inclusive package versus an independently organized trip.

NOTE: Once you've decided on your honeymoon destination and activities, fill in a new budget as accurately as possible and take it with you on your trip. Use it to chart your expenses as they occur so you will have a visual guide of whether or not you are staying within budget.

If you find that you are going over your budget, take a look at those top priority items that you'd still like to keep. See if you can eliminate some lower priority items to free up some money for the favored ones.

If you find you are under budget, celebrate with a special "gift" for yourselves (massages, an extravagant dinner, another afternoon of jet skiing, etc.).

*T*IPPING *G*UIDE

This guide is provided to help you get familiar with customary gratuity standards you may encounter throughout your travels.

Tipping customs vary from country to country. It is advisable to inquire about tipping with the international tourism board representing the country you'll be traveling in. Simply ask for information about tipping customs and social expectations. You will also want to discuss gratuities with your travel agent or planner. Some travel packages include gratuities in the total cost, some leave that to the guests, and some even discourage tipping (usually because they have built it into the total package price) Be sure to discuss this with your travel planner.

SERVICE	GRATUITY
AIR TRAVEL	
Skycaps	$1.00 per bag
Flight Attendants	none
ROAD TRAVEL	
Taxi Drivers	15% of fare (no less than 50 cents)
Limousine Driver	usually included in bill
Valet Parking	$1.00
Tour Bus Guide	$1.00
RAIL TRAVEL	
Redcaps	$1.00 per bag (or posted rate plus 50 cents)
Sleeping Car Attendant	$1.00 per person
Train Conductor and Crew	none
Dining Car Attendant	15% of bill
CRUISE	
Cabin Steward	2.5-7.5% of fare (paid at the end of the trip)
Dining Room Waiter	2.5-7.5% of fare (paid at the end of the trip)
Cabin Boy, Bar Steward, Wine Steward	5-7.5% of total fare (divided among them)

RESTAURANTS	
Maitre d', Headwaiter	none (unless special services provided, then typically $5.00)
Waiter/Waitress	15% of bill (pre tax total)
Bartender	15% of bill
Wine Steward	15% of bill
Washroom Attendant	25-50 cents
Coat Check Attendant	$1.00 for 1 or 2 coats
(NOTE: Some restaurants in foreign countries add the gratuity and/or service charge to your bill. If it has not been added, tip the customary regional rate.)	
HOTEL / RESORT	
Concierge	$2.00-10.00 for special attention or arrangements
Doorman	$1.00 for hailing taxi
Bellhop	$1.00 per bag 50 cents for showing room
Room Service	15% of bill
Chamber Maid	$1.00-2.00 per day or $5.00-10.00 per week for longer stays (no tip for one night stays)
Pool Attendant	50 cents for towel service

MISCELLANEOUS	
Barbershop	15% of cost
Beauty Salon	15% of cost
Manicure	$1.00-5.00 depending on cost of service
Facial	15% of cost
Massage	15% of cost

Things To Pack

TRAVELERS' FIRST AID KIT:

Consider the differences in the climates of where you live now and where you'll be visiting. Also consider the air conditions of airplanes, trains and boats. Bring along items that will help in the transition and keep you feeling as comfortable as possible.

- ❑ *Aspirin*
- ❑ *Antacid tablets*
- ❑ *Diarrhea medication*
- ❑ *Cold remedies/ sinus decongestant*
- ❑ *Throat lozenges*
- ❑ *Antiseptic Lotion*
- ❑ *Band-Aids*
- ❑ *Moleskin for blisters*
- ❑ *Breath mints*
- ❑ *Chapstick*
- ❑ *Insect Repellent, Insect Bite*
- ❑ *Medication*
- ❑ *Sunblock and Sunburn Relief Lotion*
- ❑ *Dry Skin Lotion/Hand Cream*
- ❑ *Eye Drops or Eye Lubricant*
- ❑ *Saline nasal spray, moisturizing nasal spray*
- ❑ *Vitamins*

❑ *Prescription drugs*
   NOTE: These should be kept in their original pharmacy containers which provide both drug and doctor information. Be sure to note the drug's generic name. You will want to pack these in your carry on baggage in case the bags you've checked become lost or delayed.

❑ *Condoms or prescription birth control*

❑ *Physicians' names, addresses, and telephone numbers*

❑ *Health Insurance phone numbers* NOTE: Be sure to contact your provider to find out about coverage while traveling in the U.S. and abroad.

❑ *Names and phone numbers of people to contact in case of an emergency.*

PACKING CHECKLIST

CARRY ON BAGGAGE:

- ☐ Travelers' First Aid Kit (see above)
- ☐ Wallet (credit cards, traveler's checks)
- ☐ Jewelry and other sentimental and valuable items that you feel you *must* bring
- ☐ Identification (Passport, Driver's License or Photo ID)
- ☐ Photocopies of the following Important Documents:
- ☐ Hotel/resort street address, phone number, written confirmation of arrangements and reservations
- ☐ Complete travel itinerary
- ☐ Airline tickets
- ☐ Name, address and phone number of emergency contact person(s) back home
- ☐ Medicine prescriptions (including generic names) and eyeglass prescription information (or an extra pair); list of food and drug allergies

- ❑ Phone numbers (including after-hour emergency phone numbers) for health insurance company and personal physicians

- ❑ Copy of your packing list. This will help you while packing up at the end of your trip. It will also be invaluable if a piece of your luggage gets lost, as you will know the contents that are missing.

- ❑ List of your travelers checks' serial numbers and 24 hour phone number for reporting loss or theft

- ❑ Phone numbers to the local U.S. embassy or consulate

- ❑ Any "essential" toiletries and one complete casual outfit in case checked baggage is delayed or lost

- ❑ Foreign language dictionary or translator

- ❑ Camera with film loaded

- ❑ Maps

- ❑ Phone numbers to the local US embassy or consulate

- ❑ Small bills/change (in U.S. dollars and in the appropriate foreign currency) for tipping

- ❑ Currency converter chart or pocket calculator

- ❑ Reading material

- ❑ Eyeglasses

- ❑ Contact lenses

- ❑ Contact lens cleaner

- ❑ Sunglasses

❑ Kleenex, gum, breath mints, and any over-the-counter medicine to ease travel discomfort

❑ Inflatable neck pillow (for lengthy, sit down travels)

❑ Address book and thank you notes (in case you have lots of traveling time)

❑ This Book

❑ Your Budget Sheet

Other items to carry-on ...

❑ _____

❑ _____

❑ _____

❑ _____

❑ _____

❑ _____

❑ _____

CHECKED BAGGAGE:

Clothing:

☐ *Casual wear* (Consider the number of each casual outfit item that you will need)

    ☐ shorts

    ☐ pants

    ☐ tops

    ☐ jackets/sweaters

    ☐ sweatshirts/sweatsuits

    ☐ belts

    ☐ socks

    ☐ underwear or panties & bras

    ☐ walking shoes/sandals/loafers

    ☐ _____

☐ *Athletic wear* (Consider the number of each sporting outfit item that you will need)

    ☐ shorts

    ☐ sweatpants

    ☐ tops

    ☐ sweatshirts/jackets

    ☐ swim suits

    ☐ swim suit cover-up

    ☐ aerobic activity outfit

- ❑ athletic equipment
- ❑ hats
- ❑ socks
- ❑ underwear or panties & exercise bras
- ❑ tennis/athletic shoes
- ❑ _____
- ❑ _____

❑ *Evening wear* (Consider the number of each evening outfit item that you will need)
- ❑ pants or pants/skirts/dresses
- ❑ belts
- ❑ dress shirts/blouses
- ❑ sweaters
- ❑ jackets/blazers/ties
- ❑ socks or pantyhose/slips
- ❑ underwear or panties & bras
- ❑ accessories
- ❑ shoes
- ❑ _____

❑ *Formal wear* (Consider the number of each formal outfit item that you will need)
- ❑ dress pants/suits/tuxedo

- ❑ dresses/gowns
- ❑ dresses
- ❑ accessories
- ❑ socks or pantyhose/slips
- ❑ underwear or panties & bras
- ❑ dress shoes
- ❑ _____
- ❑ _____

❑ *Other Clothing items*

- ❑ pajamas
- ❑ lingerie
- ❑ slippers
- ❑ robe
- ❑ _____
- ❑ _____

Miscellaneous items:

- ❑ An additional set of the important document photocopies as packed in your carry on
- ❑ Travel tour books, Tourism Bureau Information numbers
- ❑ Journal
- ❑ Special honeymoon gift for your new spouse

- [ ] Any romantic items or favorite accessories
- [ ] Extra film and camera batteries
- [ ] Plastic bags for dirty laundry
- [ ] Large plastic or nylon tote bag for bringing home new purchases
- [ ] Small sewing kit and safety pins
- [ ] Travel alarm clock
- [ ] Travel iron
- [ ] Lint brush
- [ ] Compact umbrella, Fold up rain slickers
- [ ] Copy of *Naughty Games for the Honeymoon ...and Beyond*, a playful book containing 50 sensual, fun and exciting games to fill your honeymoon with hot, passionate sex. Available in most bookstores or visit *www.yourbridalsuperstore.com*.
- [ ] _____
- [ ] _____

For International travel:

- [ ] Passports/visas
- [ ] Electric converters and adapter plugs
- [ ] Copy of appropriate forms showing proof of required vaccinations/inoculations
- [ ] _____
- [ ] _____

Personal Notes

INTERNATIONAL

TRAVEL

There are over 250 U.S. embassies and consulates around the world. After contacting the Tourism Bureau for the area you will be traveling to, it is also a wise idea to contact the U.S. Embassy or Consulate for that region. With assistance from both of these sources you will be able to determine the travel requirements and recommendations for your chosen travel destination. Within this section you will find numerous resources to assure all of your questions and concerns are addressed before you travel.

Call for a list of U.S. embassy and consulate locations with emergency phone numbers:
(202) 647-5225 **or visit:** http://travel.state.gov

PERSONAL NOTES

𝒫ASSPORTS AND 𝒱ISAS

Your travel agent should be able to provide you with information to adequately prepare you for your international travels. Additional information (and possibly more detailed and current information) can be obtained by contacting the appropriate sources listed in this section.

As a U.S. citizen, you generally need a passport to enter and to depart most foreign countries and to reenter the United States. Some countries also require Visas. A Visa is an endorsement by officials of a foreign country as permission to visit their country. You first need a passport in order to obtain a Visa. Inquire with the resources listed in this section for requirements of your specific destination.

As mentioned, you will be required to prove your U.S. citizenship upon reentry to the United States. If the country of your destination does not require you to possess a current passport, you will still need to produce proof of citizenship for U.S. Immigration. Items that are acceptable as proof of citizenship include a passport, a certified copy of your Birth Certificate, a Certificate of Nationalization, a Certificate of Citizenship, or a Report of Birth Abroad of a Citizen of the United States. Proof of identification can include a driver's license or a government or military identification card containing a photo or physical description.

NOTE: Your passport and airline tickets should reflect your maiden name for ease in proof of identification while traveling. Name changes can be processed after returning from the honeymoon with your marriage certificate.

Your passport will be one of the most important documents you will take with you. Contact the local U.S. Embassy immediately if your passport becomes lost or stolen. Have a photocopy of your passports' data page, date and place of issuance, and passport number to be kept with a contact person at home. You should also travel with a set of these photocopies in addition to an extra set of loose passport photos for speed in attaining a replacement.

Passports can be obtained from one of the 13 U.S. Passport Agencies (listed later in this section) or one of the thousands of authorized passport locations, such as state and federal courts as well as some U.S. Post Offices (check in the Government Listings section of your phone book).

Currently, the cost to obtain a passport is $60.00 (in person; Form DSP-11) or $40.00 (through the mail; Form DSP-82). If you have had a passport in the past, contact a passport agency to find out if you are eligible to apply through the mail. You will want to apply for your passport several months before your trip, keeping in mind that

January through July is a busier time and the process may take longer.

In addition to calling the U.S. Passport Agencies for personal assistance, you can also call their 24-hour recorded information lines for information on agency locations, travel advisories and warnings, and Consular Information Sheets pertaining to every country in the world.

Travel Advisory Updates are also available 24 hours a day by calling:

> The Department of State's Office
> of Overseas Citizens' Services at:
> (202) 647-5225

Additional, and very helpful, official information for U.S. citizens regarding international travel can be found at:
> http://travel.state.gov

Foreign embassies and consulates located in the U.S. can provide current information regarding their country. You can locate phone numbers and addresses in the following:

> *The Congressional Directory*
> *Foreign Consular Offices in the United States*
> (both available at your local library)

U.S. Passport Agencies

Boston Passport Agency
Thomas P. O'Neill Federal Building
10 Causeway Street, Suite 247
Boston, MA   02222-1094

Charleston Passport Center
1269 Holland Street
Charleston, SC   29405

Chicago Passport Agency
Kluczynski Federal Building
230 S. Dearborn Street, Suite 380
Chicago, IL   60604-1564
(312) 341-6020

Honolulu Passport Agency
First Hawaiian Tower
1132 Bishop Street, Suite 500
Honolulu, HI   96813-2809
(808) 522-8283

Houston Passport Agency
Mickey Leland Federal Building
1919 Smith Street, Suite 1400
Houston, TX   77002-8049
(713) 751-0294

Los Angeles Passport Agency
Federal Building
11000 Wilshire Boulevard, Suite 1000
Los Angeles, CA   90024-3615
(310) 575-5700

Miami Passport Agency
Claude Pepper Federal Office Building
51 SW First Avenue, 3rd Floor
Miami, FL   33130-1680
(305) 539-3600

New Orleans Passport Agency
>One Canal Place
>New Orleans, LA

New York Passport Agency
>376 Hudson Street
>New York, NY   10014
>(212) 206-3500

Philadelphia Passport Agency
>U.S. Custom House
>200 Chestnut Street, Room 103
>Philadelphia, PA   19106-2970
>(215) 418-5937

San Francisco Passport Agency
>95 Hawthorne Street, 5th Floor
>San Francisco, CA   94105-3901
>(415) 538-2700

Seattle Passport Agency
>Henry Jackson Federal Building
>915 Second Avenue, Suite 992
>Seattle, WA   98174-1091

Stamford Passport Agency
>One Landmark Square
>Stamford, CT   06901-2667
>(203) 969-9000

Washington Passport Agency
>1111 19th Street, N.W.
>Washington, D.C. 20524
>(202) 647-0518

*Some private sources offering assistance in obtaining a
passport (usually offering expedited service):*

International Visa Service
     1 (800) 627-1112
World Wide Visas
     1 (800) 527-1861
Travel Document Systems
     1 (800) 874-5100
     www.traveldocs.com

*H*EALTH *C*ONCERNS

In the United States the National Center for Infectious Diseases (NCID) and the Centers for Disease Control (CDC) provide the most current information pertinent to international travel. The World Health Organization (WHO) concerns itself with general and specific health issues for almost every part of the world. Health and safety issues as related to international travel are the basis for the International Heath Regulations adopted by the World Health Organization.

Your travel agent should be fully informed about current conditions and requirements. Your personal physician should also be able to provide you with health-related information and advice for traveling in the region you visit. You can personally obtain very useful (and very thorough) information by using the appropriate sources listed below:

Available from the Center for Disease Control and Prevention, Travelers' Health Section:

Health Information for International Travel ("The Yellow Book") available from:

> The Superintendent of Documents
> U.S. Government Printing Office
> Washington, D.C. 20402
> 202-512-1800
> or download a free copy at:
> www.cdc.gov

Summary of Health Information for International Travel ("The Blue Sheet")

> A biweekly publication
> available by fax: 404-332-4565
> (request document 220022#)

For updates and changes by phone or fax:

> (404) 332-4559 or visit: www.cdc.gov

OTHER CONCERNS

TRAVELERS' HEALTH INSURANCE COVERAGE

If your health insurance policy does not cover you abroad, consider acquiring a temporary health insurance policy. Travel agencies, health insurance companies, travelers' check companies, and your local phone book should be able to provide names of relevant companies for you. In addition to health insurance coverage, many policy packages also include protection in case of trip cancellation and baggage loss.

CUSTOMS

Keep prescription medications in their original pharmacy containers with the original labels. Bring a copy of your prescriptions and note the drug's generic name. You may consider getting a letter from your physician warranting your need for the medication.

Some useful publications regarding customs and custom policies:

Know Before You Go; Customs Hints for Returning U.S. Residents

U.S. Customs
P.O. Box 7407
Washington, D.C. 20004
202-566-8195

Travelers' Tips on Bringing Food, Plant and Animal Products into the United States
U.S. Department of Agriculture
613 Federal Building
6505 Belcrest Road
Hyattsville, MD 20782

An Unwanted Souvenir; Lead in Ceramic Ware
U.S. Food and Drug Administration
HFI-40
Rockville, MD 20857

*T*HINGS TO DO
FOR YOUR HONEYMOON

DONE
✓

*T*HINGS TO DO

FOR YOUR HONEYMOON

DONE
✓

THINGS TO DO

FOR YOUR HONEYMOON

DONE
√

Things to do

FOR YOUR HONEYMOON

DONE
✓

PERSONAL NOTES

Personal Notes

PERSONAL NOTES

Personal Notes

Wedding Solutions Publishing
proudly presents...

YOUR BRIDAL
SUPERSTORE
...everything but the groom™

www.YourBridalSuperstore.com

...offering a complete collection of the most
beautiful and elegant wedding accessories, jewelry
and invitations available. Find everything you need
for your wedding in one convenient location!

Also featuring...
Advice from Wedding Planning Experts
Tips To Save Money
On-line classified section
Chat Room
and much more!

See the following *Wedding Checklist* for a list of
some of the items currently available at
www.YourBridalSuperstore.com

FREE
valuable wedding gift
with your first order

For details, log on to:
www.YourBridalSuperstore.com

~ Wedding Checklist ~

Wedding Stationery

- ☐ Invitations
- ☐ Announcements
- ☐ Reception Enclosures
- ☐ Respond Card /Envelopes
- ☐ At Home Cards
- ☐ Programs
- ☐ Bookmarks
- ☐ Bows, Ribbons, and Wraps
- ☐ Thank You Notes
- ☐ Calligraphy Pens
- ☐ Pew Cards
- ☐ Decorative Seals
- ☐ Lined Inner Envelopes
- ☐ Printed Envelopes

Wedding Party Gifts

- ☐ Personalized Glassware and Flask
- ☐ Keepsake Box
- ☐ Rich Vanilla Candle
- ☐ Jewelry Heart Box
- ☐ Flower Girl T-shirt & Coloring Book
- ☐ Ring Bearer T-shirt & Coloring Book

YOUR BRIDAL SUPERSTORE
...everything but the groom™

www.YourBridalSuperstore.com

Ceremony Essentials

- ☐ Aisle Runner, Pew Bows
- ☐ Unity Candle
- ☐ Taper Candles
- ☐ Flower Girl Basket
- ☐ Ring Bearer Pillow or Chest
- ☐ Bridal Handbag
- ☐ Garters
- ☐ Guest Book
- ☐ Plume Pen
- ☐ Gratuity Envelopes

Reception Essentials

- ☐ Cake Knife & Server
- ☐ Tissue Bells, Paper Streamers
- ☐ Cake Boxes or Bags
- ☐ Book or Box Matches
- ☐ Favor Making Supplies
- ☐ Candy Hearts
- ☐ Balloons
- ☐ Place Cards
- ☐ Ribbon Pulling Charms
- ☐ Bouquet Holders
- ☐ Cookie Cutter Favors
- ☐ Favor Ribbons
- ☐ Candy Bar Wrapper Favors
- ☐ Glass Candle Favors

YOUR BRIDAL
SUPERSTORE
...everything but the groom™
www.YourBridalSuperstore.com

Reception Essentials (cont.d)

- ☐ Cake Tops
- ☐ Cake Top Domes
- ☐ Floating Candles & Glass Cylinder
- ☐ Favor Bells
- ☐ Thank You Ribbons, Scrolls & Bookmarks
- ☐ Wishing Well Card Holder
- ☐ Toasting Glasses/Goblets
- ☐ Sequined Heart or Chiffon Tie-Ons
- ☐ Biodegradable Heart-Shaped Rice
- ☐ Wedding Bubbles
- ☐ Seeds of Love
- ☐ "Just Married" Banner

Special Items

- ☐ Parents' Gifts
- ☐ Memories Box
- ☐ Marriage Certificate
- ☐ Thank You Guide
- ☐ Personalized License Plate
- ☐ Car Decorating Kit
- ☐ Glass Chalk
- ☐ Bridal Gown Cover
- ☐ Video Case
- ☐ Wedding Time Capsule

YOUR BRIDAL SUPERSTORE
...everything but the groom™